Kingdoms of Magic

Royal Betrayals

Trademark ™ 2014 Kingdoms Of Magic :**Denaye McKoy**

ISBN-13: 978-0692235515 (Custom Universal)

ISBN-10: 0692235515

Edited By CreateSpace Editing

Fantasy, Fiction novel

Contents

Dedication

I dedicate this book to Ms. Lori Goldman, Mrs. Helene Weinshraub, and Mrs. Kim Ostrowski, my teachers and guidance counselor from Hightstown High School. They are three amazing teachers that greatly inspired me, always giving me their undivided attention, and making this book possible.

Thank you as well to all the fans of the Kingdoms of Magic series.

Prologue

Chapter 1

Once upon a time, there were seven
kingdoms, named Balcot, Viel, Euselus (u-
sell-us), Nivera, Madoness, Wathe, and Zaru.
All the kingdoms got along except for Wathe,
which kept everything that went on in the
kingdom inside their kingdom walls. No one
came in or out of the kingdom. But the
kingdom that we're going to talk about is
Zaru. The Kingdom of Zaru was a beautiful
palace that sat on a hilltop surrounded by
water. Inside the palace lived a beautiful
sixteen-year-old princess named Lillianna;
her father, forty-year-old King Joseph; and
her mother, forty-year-old Queen Tianna.

The royal families of every kingdom did not have last names like the villagers. But if they were addressed with one, then their kingdom name was their last name.

King Joseph was a man who needed everything done correctly. He had short red hair and a weird mustache. Queen Tianna was very quiet, but when she spoke she had everyone's attention. She had beautiful, long, blond hair, but she always kept her hair up in different gorgeous updos. She also had beautiful blue eyes, as blue as the sky. Lillianna had gorgeous red hair that women were jealous of and eyes as beautiful as her mother's. Lillianna's beauty was beyond that of any regular girl, and people despised her because of it. Lillianna was the type of girl who always did what her parents told her to, and she always did as others told her to, until now.

They lived in a great palace with wonderful servants, but Lillianna didn't feel the same way. She hated living in the palace. Even though she got everything she wanted, she was still very unhappy and hated that she couldn't make her own decisions. So one day, Lillianna decided to leave the palace and ran into the forest. As she was running, Lillianna was paying so much attention to what might be behind her, wondering if anyone was following her, that she ran into what appeared to be an old ugly man. The old man promised to help her to have a place to live and be much happier than living with her parents. He had a very dark demeanor to him. He was tall and wore a black cloak. He was not the most beautiful person you've ever seen, but Lillianna decided to go with the man. They walked for many hours through the forest and got to this huge, old palace with rusty gates. The sky was grayer on this side of the kingdom. This side of the kingdom was strange to her; the trees were dead and so were the flowers. As Lillianna was walking in, it was cold and the castle looked like it was falling apart. Then she heard a sound. Lillianna looked back and the old man was gone. She was by herself in a dark place.

Lillianna then heard a noise up the stairs, so she kept on walking toward it. The sound kept on getting louder and louder and louder, as she walked closer and closer. Then she got to a room that had torn blinds, faded paint on the walls, and the floor was dirty. She walked in and saw a man. Lillianna walked closer to him and said hi to him and got no response back. Then she took another step and he yelled angrily, "Who are you, and what are you doing here?" She told him her name was Lillianna and that she was the princess from the other side of the kingdom. His voice then calmed down and he seemed really happy to see her. They went to another room and sat for tea. This room looked a lot better than the last room, but not like what she was used to. He asked her if she was the daughter of King Joseph and also asked a lot of questions about the palace. She told him King Joseph was her father and answered all the questions honestly. After dinner, he showed her to a beautiful room to sleep with a big bed, couch, and balcony. From the outside of the palace Lillianna didn't think there would be a nice room in the palace. So she decided to stay. The next day she would finish viewing the kingdom and return home.

Later that night, someone came into Lillianna's guest chambers and knocked her out by placing a cloth over her face, with chloroform on it. Lillianna later woke up tied up in the dungeon. She didn't know what to do, so she began to cry and wished she never ran away. All of a sudden Lillianna saw a woman. Lillianna asked the woman "Who are you?"
The woman told her that her name was Ramina, and then behind her she saw the old man that led her there. The old man raised his voice to Ramina to be quiet before they decide to tell Lillianna anything. The old man turned out to be very greedy. He asked Lillianna to promise to give them riches, and also that King Joseph wouldn't hurt them if they let her go. Lillianna agreed, and Ramina told her the story. Ramina explained, "The man who showed you to your room was your brother, Prince Zalem, the rightful heir to the

throne." Ramina was a maid that always helped Prince Zalem.

The old man explained, "I was never trying to put you in danger. I was headed to Zaru to bring you to the Prince." Prince Zalem's mother always told him that his father, King Joseph, never wanted him. Prince Zalem wanted to take the title of King back. Lillianna begged Ramina to let her go, and she forgave them for everything, even for not stopping Prince Zalem. They both decided to let her go. Lillianna rushed back to the palace with Ramina and the old man by her side. When Lillianna arrived there was a huge war and Lillianna couldn't do much. Prince Zalem brought the people that were banished to help him fight. Lillianna searched for her father but couldn't find him. She then decided to go and find her mother. Lillianna searched all over the palace, up and down many stairs. Finally, a servant named Isabelle told Lillianna her mother was in her chambers. Lillianna burst through the doors of the chambers to find her mother outside on her balcony, watching the war. Lillianna called for her mother, and she turned and ran to her. The Queen was so happy to see her daughter. Queen Tianna was worried about Lillianna, but so glad she was in her arms and OK.

The Queen then asked, "Where were you?" Lillianna told her mother, "I was at the old abandoned palace." Her mother looked at her in shock, and Lillianna continued to explain why the war was going on and that Zalem was King Joseph's son.

Queen Tianna was in amazement to hear that, because she had never heard of Zalem. The Queen then looked behind her and saw two strangers. The Queen then asked her daughter, "Lillianna, who are these people?" Lillianna replied, "They helped me get out of the abandoned palace, but don't worry about them. Please let's go and try to stop this war."

Queen Tianna replied, "I agree, but how, Lillianna?" None of them knew how, but they all agreed that they couldn't do anything by staying in her chambers. They quickly went outside.

When Lillianna finally got outside, she saw her father and her brother about to go head-to-head and she yelled, "Stop!"

Both of them stopped, with King Joseph's sword at Zalem's neck. They both looked at her as she walked closer to them and then disarmed them. Lillianna told her father that the guy underneath the armor was Prince Zalem, the heir to the throne, and his son. King Joseph was in a great deal of shock. He dropped his sword and shield. He didn't believe that he could have had a son and not know him. The King then walked over to the boy and took Zalem's helmet off. The boy looked just like him. He had red hair, and his eyes looked very familiar to the King. Prince Zalem was upset with him and he didn't believe that King Joseph didn't know anything about him. His mother had told him when he was a child that his father didn't want him. Then Zalem said, "When I was a baby you denied me; the woman that raised me told me."

King Joseph assured him that he never knew of him and if he had, then Prince Zalem would have lived in the palace as royalty. King Joseph recognized his eyes but couldn't put everything together in his head to make sense. The King wanted to get to know the boy, so he asked him if he wanted to stay in the palace and let them figure everything out. Lillianna wanted him to agree and just move in, and so did Queen Tianna. Prince Zalem agreed, as long as Ramina and the old man could come as well.

Lillianna agreed, but the old man would have to give his name. The old man answered, "You'll know in good time...but for now, call me Cloak."

Chapter 2

It was a beautiful day in Zaru. When
Lillianna awoke, she remembered meeting
her brother like it was yesterday, although it
had already been a week. Lillianna had been
assured that Zalem was her brother, even
though King Joseph was afraid to confront
Zalem. King Joseph didn't explain much to
Lillianna, but she knew in good time she
would understand. Lillianna realized that
she hadn't spent much time getting to know
Zalem. So she decided to take Zalem to one
of her favorite places. When Lillianna needed
a quiet place to think or read, she took a

walk outside the palace, to the lake. They both went there together, and she prepared a picnic for them. Lillianna decided to ask Zalem about his childhood and how it was when he grew up. Prince Zalem explained that his mother didn't have much; they lived as poor people do. He never got birthday presents, but his mother did all she could to make sure he had fun. Lillianna felt so bad for him because on her birthdays she got more presents than what could be held in her bed chamber.

Lillianna now understood that Zalem's mother meant everything to him. She asked what happened to his mother. Zalem explained that his mother had to leave for business and Cloak would have to take care of him when she was gone. Lillianna started to feel that she understood her brother a lot better. She felt so sorry that they didn't grow up together, but moved past it so she could get to know him now. Deep down, she knew that he would be an amazing brother to her.

Later that evening, Prince Zalem returned to his bed chamber, where Ramina was waiting for him. Prince Zalem told Ramina that the plan was in motion. Ramina answered Zalem, asking, "Do they believe that you're pristine?" Prince Zalem told Ramina that they did not suspect him at all and didn't know that she was his mother. Ramina was so excited.

Zalem asked her, "When should we put the plan in effect?"

Ramina answered, "There is a change in the plan; I want to first capture Joseph, Tianna, and Lillianna."

Zalem did not agree that they should be kidnapped. He didn't really want to do this, but Ramina goaded him on. He didn't have the heart to say no, so he went along with the plan.

While Zalem was with Ramina brewing their plan, the King was trying to figure out a way to confront Zalem. So he went to talk to his wife, Tianna. "I have realized who Zalem looks like, and I don't understand how my late wife could have had a child," said King Joseph.

Queen Tianna replied, "You'll never know

unless you confront him." The King agreed and decided that first thing in the morning he would go and meet him. That night, the King nervously tossed and turned.

The next day, the kingdom awoke to hear of a meeting in the main hall. The message said that King Joseph was supposed to meet the townspeople and everyone in the palace in the main hall. When everyone arrived, Queen Tianna and Princess Lillianna couldn't find King Joseph. Zalem was nowhere to be found, as well. "Your father might be with Zalem. They are supposed to be talking about his late mother."
Lillianna turned to her mother, puzzled, and said, "Late? She's not dead. She raised Zalem and he told me that himself at the lake." The Queen was confused, but couldn't think about that. She was about to leave the hall, when Ramina went up to the public to speak. Ramina began to explain that the Kingdom would soon be seeing a new King. Lillianna and the Queen realized that King Joseph was welcoming Prince Zalem into the

kingdom. Zalem walked passed Tianna and Lillianna onto the platform.

Cloak then grabbed Tianna quietly, and he tied her up while Lillianna was peeking up from underneath the platform. He quietly tied up Lillianna as well. They realized that what they thought was going on, wasn't. While Cloak was dragging the Queen and Princess to the dungeon, Lillianna's eyes and Zalem's eyes met. She looked at him with such shame and tears. But none of the guests saw them get dragged away. The King feared for his family and went up on the platform. He told the people to listen to Zalem, and that he would be stepping down as King. Ramina then told the people to give up their money or anything of value, and that she was their ruler.

The King went underneath the platform to Cloak and demanded to see his family. "You took me away from my family this morning and held me against my will. I did what you wanted, now I want to see my family," said the King. Cloak took him to the dungeon, where he was tricked into a cell, not knowing where his family was. The King, Queen, and Princess were scared for their lives, so close but so far from one another.

Zalem couldn't sleep that night, remembering the look in Lillianna's eyes. He then decided to go and visit Lillianna. When he got there, Lillianna wasn't in the mood to speak. Zalem tried to apologize and even admitted that he was planning to kidnap their father, but Ramina went overboard with kidnapping her and Tianna, and taking everyone's money. He also explained that Ramina was his mother and the Queen. Lillianna chased him away and told him she'd never forgive him. She also told him to never call King Joseph his father, because he never deserved anything. Zalem was crushed. He hoped his mother was happy and that this was all worth it.

After seeing Lillianna in the dungeon, Zalem decided to go and visit his mother, who had already started to remodel the palace. Ramina told Zalem how proud she was of him and that she wanted to tell him something.

"OK, you have my full attention," said Zalem. "I don't want you worrying about running the Kingdom. I want Cloak to help me run the Kingdom, and you make all the appearances. I figured that you don't know much and you could use my help," Ramina insisted.

"I don't know," said Zalem. But when he looked at his mother's face, he could not say no. He then agreed to let them lead Zaru.

"I think you made a great decision," said Ramina, smiling, as Cloak then walked in. One of the guards was right there as well, so Zalem informed them that Ramina would be in charge. "Now, can you please go and check on the prisoners, and let Cloak and I have some privacy?" said Ramina.

Zalem had just come from seeing the prisoners, so he decided he was going to act like he was going, but wasn't. Ramina walked Zalem out the door and watched him walk away. Then she looked both ways and shut the door.

While Zalem hid where he could listen to them speaking and not be seen. Ramina gave Cloak a kiss on the lips and told him that they had it all.

"That boy is so stupid. He did everything you asked him," said Cloak.

"Yes, and he really thinks I am his mother, not knowing I stole him," said Ramina.

Zalem couldn't believe what he was hearing and was filled with anger. He was so filled with anger that he didn't know what to do with it. Even so, he tried to keep composed and keep on listening.

"And where did you get that stupid name from? CLOAK!" asked Ramina.

"I couldn't tell the King I was his younger brother Lathem, who always wanted what he had," said Cloak.

Zalem felt so dumb for even going along with the plan, and now was wondering who he was, or who he could trust. Prince Zalem barged into the room, demanding to know who he truly was. Lathem told him that he was the King's son but Zalem's true mother passed away years ago. When Zalem was born, his mother was very sick and left Lathem the baby to give to King Joseph. But that never happened.

Ramina decided that Zalem had heard too much and had to be locked up until they were ready for everyone to know who he was. Zalem was thrown in the dungeon far away from Lillianna, the King, and Queen, so he couldn't warn them of what was going on.

Lathem decided to go down to the dungeon, dressed as Cloak, to see King Joseph and wanted to talk about old times. King Joseph didn't wish to see anyone but his daughter and wife. As long as they were OK, he didn't care much about anyone else. Lathem began to talk about when he used to live in the palace. King Joseph didn't know what Lathem was talking about. Lathem took off his mustache, but the King still did not recognize who he was. Lathem explained how Joseph always got everything he wanted because he was going to be King, and Lathem never got anything.

King Joseph then realized that Cloak was his little brother Lathem. He was so upset that his brother had done this to him. The King then turned to his brother and asked him

"Why?"

Lathem explained that he hated the way he was treated, and he wanted to run the Kingdom. The King didn't understand why his brother left in the first place. Lathem could have come to Joseph and told him and they would have run the Kingdom together. Lathem didn't expect his brother to say that to him.

"I always loved you, Lathem, but I'm sad to see you come to a point where I can't trust you," said the King.

Lathem now felt that he let his brother down and he shouldn't have done that. "I will always love you, big brother," said Lathem. He slowly walked away with his head down.

Lathem decided to go to Ramina and see if she would reconsider. Ramina wouldn't hear it, but because she loved Lathem she gave him a second chance and warned him not to do anything to betray her. Lathem wouldn't listen to her, but decided to act like everything was OK with him and Ramina. He then chose to go to Prince Zalem and figure out a way to get the kingdom back. After

their talk, Lathem let Zalem out of his cell
and told him to rescue Lillianna, while he
would rescue The Queen and King and bring
them to Lillianna's cell.

King Joseph was lying down in his cell,
worried about his wife. Then all of a sudden
he heard her voice. He thought he was going
crazy, but when he got up and turned
around he was shocked to see his wife in
front of him again. He grabbed her and
hugged her tight in his arms.

On the other side of the dungeon, Lillianna
didn't want to go anywhere with Zalem.
Zalem begged her and explained all about
Ramina and Cloak; that Cloak was their
Uncle Lathem. He explained how King
Joseph was truly his father as well. She
realized that Lathem was the brother that
her father always spoke of. Lillianna knew it
was the truth. Lillianna hugged Zalem and
asked to see her father. Just as she said that
King Joseph and Queen Tianna appeared.
When King Joseph saw his daughter, he was
overwhelmed. He hugged both of his
children, at the same time and wouldn't let

them go. Now they had to figure out a way to get back their kingdom.

But Ramina was already on to them and was headed down to the dungeon. Ramina was going to kill Lathem for betraying her wishes.

Chapter 3

One of the guards saw Zalem and Lathem
letting everyone out of their cells and went
and told Ramina. Ramina was filled with
anger and was going to destroy Lathem.
They all went into Lillianna's cell, and
Lathem apologized to the entire family.
Lathem was sorry for what he had done, but
explained that Zalem was truly the heir to
the throne. King Joseph told Zalem, "Your
mother's name was Eliza, and she was an
amazing woman. Eliza and I were married
before I had Lillianna or married Queen
Tianna. Ramina was Queen Eliza's caregiver

while I was gone out of town for business. Eliza delivered our beautiful baby boy and then passed away soon after. Ramina thought of a plan to hide the baby and not tell me, so that she and Lathem would raise you. When I returned home, I was ashamed of myself for not being there. I was even more distraught to see my wife dead, with my unborn child. Then soon after Ramina left, Lathem vanished and no one saw or heard from him again."

Lathem apologized and said that he never thought Ramina would go so far to hurt everyone. King Joseph then said, "I was so upset with you, Lathem, but I can look at my son and I am filled with joy." He was overjoyed that a piece of Eliza still lived on. Lathem promised he would work hard to be worthy of their trust again.

Lillianna didn't know who to trust, and the Queen tried to comfort her husband, but she was puzzled. She knew Ramina before, but couldn't believe she would do this.

Before Eliza died, she told Lathem that she wanted a baby boy, and his name to be

Zalem, but if it was a girl it would be Elizabeth. Zalem didn't know what to say, because he was lied to his entire life. His whole childhood and everything was taken away from him. The worst part was to know his own Uncle and Ramina were the ones to take it away from him. They were the people that took care of him and raised him, and the people that he thought would always be there to protect him.

Now Lathem had to figure out a way to get them out of the dungeon. He told everyone to follow him, but King Joseph didn't wish to. Queen Tianna believed in Lathem and decided to follow him, so they decided to follow her in accordance. On their way up the stairs, they heard Ramina coming down the stairs, venting. Lathem guided them down the stairs quickly and quietly. They hid tightly behind the stairs around the corner. Lathem ran up the stairs quickly after leaving them around the corner and met up with Ramina. Lathem asked Ramina what she was doing coming down to the dungeon. Ramina told Lathem that she

was going to check on them because one of
the guards advised her to come down.
Lathem told her he was headed upstairs to
help her remodel. Ramina wanted Lathem to
go downstairs with her, and Lathem did as
she wished. When they both got downstairs
they went the opposite direction than where
Zalem, Lillianna, the Queen, and the King
were hiding. As soon as they walked down
the hall, the four of them slipped by quickly
and went up the stairs, where one of the
guards saw them. When they saw the guard,
they went running in the other direction. The
guard stopped them and assured them that
he was on their side. He hated Ramina and
told them he would help them get out of the
palace.

Meanwhile, Ramina discovered that Zalem,
Lillianna, Queen Tianna, and King Joseph
had all escaped. Ramina was so upset and
realized that Lathem was the last person
downstairs to see them. She believed that he
was the one to help them get out. But when
Ramina turned around, he was gone.
Ramina instructed the guards to find

everyone but Lathem. She would find him herself, not knowing that Lathem had been hiding in the dungeon the entire time. Lathem had no idea how to get out or where his family was.

Upstairs, the guard was leading them to safety. He had figured out a plan to dress them up in guard uniforms. No one would suspected them. The guard took them to a private room to change, and told them to follow him outside to safety. Ramina ran upstairs and stopped them in their tracks as they were walking through the palace. She told them that the King, Queen, Prince and Princess were missing, not knowing that the guards in front of her were them. The main guard took Ramina's instructions, but ignored them by leading everyone to safety outside the palace.

Lillianna asked the guard, "What is your name?"

He replied, "My name is Zion Blackmore." He explained that he was a new guard, and he missed when King Joseph was in command, and that Ramina treated everyone terribly.

Zion was a young, strong guard. He had brown hair with hazel eyes and was well built.

The family was so grateful to him for leading them to safety. Lillianna gave him a kiss on the cheek and said, "Thank you." They both smiled at one another, and then she ran off into the canoe, where her parents and brother sat, waiting for her. Zion told them to go to the old log cabin until he came for them.

Before they went off too far, King Joseph told Zion to watch over brother Lathem and put Ramina in the dungeon.

While they were escaping, in the castle Lathem had to figure out how to get out of the dungeon. He felt ashamed that he let Ramina get this far, to get him to betray his family. Those people were the ones that truly loved him. Lathem remembered how beautiful the palace was that he grew up in and then he looked around. It was sad to see how he had destroyed it. Lathem then realized that he had to go and confront Ramina. He needed to do it sooner, rather than later. There was no reason for him to run, because this is where he truly belonged. Lathem walked up the dungeon stairs, through the hallway to the main hall. Then he reached the kitchen, where he found Ramina. Ramina was upset with Lathem and couldn't understand, but was wondering at the same time why he betrayed her. Lathem told her that it was wrong of her to go and take the townspeople's money and to kidnap the Queen, King, Prince, and Princess. He was ashamed of the woman she had become, and he wanted the woman she was to come back.

He said, "Ramina, why? You know I would do anything for you. I even ran away and left my family to be with you. You knew my father didn't want us to be together because you were a servant. So I walked away, and you destroyed everything."

Ramina thought that this was what he wanted, so that he could become king. Lathem explained to Ramina that he did not want to become king the way she would do it. Ramina was going to hurt Lathem, then she saw that behind him was a guard about to attack him. Ramina was concentrating so much on the guard behind Lathem, and playing the part of the loving girlfriend, that she didn't see Zion behind her, ready to arrest her. Zion grabbed her first, and then the other guard went over to help put her in chains. Lathem was hurt to see the guard pull the knife from behind her back that she was going to use to kill him. Lathem watched as they took Ramina back to the dungeon and gave her a kiss good-bye. He then told her he wished that it had never come to this. Lathem now had to find his family. Zion knew where they were, and told him they were safe and that he would see them later. Lathem was relieved that everyone was OK.

Later that afternoon, after dealing with Ramina, Lathem and Zion went into another canoe to get the King and his family. When Lathem saw all of them alive, he was overjoyed. Lillianna gave Zion an unplanned passionate kiss and a huge hug. They all went back to the Kingdom, where King Joseph took his place back as King. The

Queen and King decided to name Lathem as
the most helpful advisor, who helped the
king make all the decisions. Zion and
Lillianna were now dating as well, and Zion
became head of the guards. Zalem moved
into the kingdom, where he would be trained
to become King and take over the entire
kingdom.

The Beginning:

Chapter 4

Once again in Zaru, Prince Zalem was getting ready for Princess Lillianna's early May wedding. Everything was done according to Lillianna's perfect touch. The cake was white with five layers and had yellow flowers holding together each ribbon at the bottom of every layer of the cake. The cake was made from a special recipe that stayed in the family. It also had silver lining above each ribbon and in the middle of each flower's stamens. It was all edible.
Lillianna had beautiful yellow roses and white lilies in her bouquet, and the beautiful crown that belonged to her grandmother

when she was princess. Lillianna was so excited to be marrying Zion.

Prince Zalem was so excited for his sister, but quickly realized that soon he would have to pick a bride, who would be known as Zaru's Queen. He suddenly got nervous and headed to the courtyard. Everyone was headed to the courtyard, where the wedding was to take place. Right before the wedding, Zion wanted to meet with all of the groomsmen. He made a speech explaining that he truly appreciated everyone and everything they had done to help Lillianna and him to be able to get married. Zion thanked King Joseph for giving his blessing for the two of them to be wed. On the right of the King was Lathem, and Zion thanked him for being loyal to them and helping to put the family back together. To the right of Zion was his older brother, twenty-two-year-old Ethan, who he thanked for helping him to be the man he is today. Ethan was the one who raised Zion when his father passed away. To Ethan's right was the ring bearer, their little brother

Charles. Zion gave him a hug and told him that he was very special to him. Finally, Zion got to Zalem and thanked him for giving him peace of mind and a great wedding day with Lillianna.

While the men were in the courtyard, Lillianna's mother and two servants, Isabelle and Rose, were helping Lillianna to get dressed and do her hair and makeup. Rose was Queen Tianna's servant and Isabelle's mother. Isabelle would come and help Rose in the palace when she needed help. Lillianna's mother made sure to get everything for the wedding. Something old and borrowed was her grandmother's wedding crown, but she didn't have anything new or blue. So Isabelle helped Queen Tianna get something blue and new, and it was wrapped up in a beautiful box. Queen Tianna asked Isabelle to bring Lillianna's present. Lillianna hugged Isabelle and gave her mother a kiss and thanked them both for the present. Lillianna opened it and told her mother, "It's beautiful." It was a gorgeous pair of diamond earrings with a matching necklace and a bracelet that was engraved in blue on the side that would lie on her skin. The engraving said "Special Young Lady." Her mother explained that she picked that because she always thought of Lillianna as special to her.

Isabelle was happy to do something for her because she was Lillianna's best friend. Lillianna loved when Isabelle and Rose spent time with her. Rose smiled as she stood in the corner and felt like it was her own daughter getting married.

Lillianna finally got into her dress but wanted to speak to someone before she married Zion. She called for her brother Zalem, and Rose went down to the courtyard to get him. Lillianna was pacing in her chambers waiting for Prince Zalem and was talking to her new dog, Royal, who was a beautiful black shihtzu that had been a gift from Zion. Then, suddenly, Zalem walked through the door and Lillianna was relieved to see him. Zalem walked over to Lillianna and said "You look gorgeous...but you wished to see me?"

Lillianna responded "Yes!" as she twirled around to let him see the dress and then said, "Have a seat please." She pushed him down into the seat and began pacing again. Lillianna looked so beautiful in her white dress with her mother's partial lace veil. Her dress was long and had a beautiful long train. At the bottom of the dress, encrusted in the design of her veil and train, were silver and diamonds. The dress had short sleeves that lay off her shoulders, and the sleeves were lined with silver as well. Lillianna was one of the prettiest brides, and the jewelry her mother gave her topped it off. Her hair was put in a high updo, and her grandmother's wedding crown was placed on her head. Throughout the updo, diamonds were placed. The veil reached fingertip length and attached on top of her head behind the headband where the updo began. Her cheeks were touched with a little rouge and a beautiful concealer that matched her skin perfectly. She didn't need much makeup because she was so beautiful.

Lillianna asked Zalem if he would help her to

present a gift to their father at the reception. Zalem agreed that he would, and she asked him to go down the main hall with her, where the wedding party waited for her. As they walked out the door to her chambers, Rose and Isabelle were there to lift her dress. Prince Zalem brought her to their father. King Joseph kissed his daughter on her cheek and he pulled the veil over her face As he did, he told her she looked beautiful. Isabelle was her maid of honor and Ethan was Zion's best man. Zion was at the altar, awaiting his bride. First down the aisle was Zalem and Rose. The aisle was a white carpet with the kingdom's crest on it. After that came Isabelle and Ethan, and then Charles, Royal, and the flower girls. Finally, it was time for King Joseph to join Lillianna at the top of the aisle and everyone stood up. On the right of the altar the groom's family was seated and to the left was the bride's family. Now it was time for Princess Lillianna to make her way down the aisle to the altar. The aisle was lined with flower petals, and by each chair that ended and began each row, there was a flower arrangement of white lilies and yellow roses hanging from a black hook.

When Lillianna reached the front where the platform was, Zion told her that she looked beautiful, and she laughed. They stood under a gorgeous flower arch and Lillianna's bridesmaids stood on her side of the aisle. The groomsmen stood on Zion's side. They were arranged in a diagonal line, so they could look at the bride and groom and the guests as well. During the entire service Zalem was looking Isabelle's way. Zalem always used to believe that servants were nothing more than servants, yet Lillianna let Isabelle sit like royalty.

Later that evening when the reception came along, Zalem got to meet a lot of family that he never knew existed. The King went up and revealed his gift to the bride and groom: he would be sending them on their honeymoon to his island. After he stood up, Lillianna grabbed her father quickly and asked Zalem to come up to help. Then Zalem, Zion, and Lillianna presented King

Joseph with a solid gold chalice. She then said, "This is in honor of being his three children, soon to be four." Lillianna winked at Zalem, hoping for someone soon to be by his side.

There were a lot of women trying to meet Zalem and ask him to dance. After about two hours of being tugged left and right, Zalem was exhausted. As he was headed to sit, he saw Isabelle sitting, laughing at a drunken old man dancing, or at least trying to dance. Zalem gripped the chair next to her and asked Isabelle if he could sit down next to her. Then a servant came running to pull out Zalem's chair. Zalem quickly but nicely told the man that he didn't need his assistance, as he pulled out his own chair. Isabelle began a conversation with Zalem and said, "I think her feet hurt more than yours." They both stared at a woman's feet stuffed into her shoes, and they laughed.
"I never thought I would stop dancing with her," said Zalem. They laughed again calmly and then they became silent, as he gazed at

his sister and how happy she was on the dance floor. Then he glanced at his father and Queen Tianna and saw how happy he was. He wanted to be that happy when he married his queen.

Isabelle noticed him gazing at them, and she decided to try to snap him out of it. "She looks so happy," said Isabelle, as she looked at Lillianna.

Zalem nodded his head in agreement. "I hope to be happy like that one day...Lillianna is truly my best friend, and I am happy for her." Zalem glanced at Isabelle and asked, "How was life growing up around the palace?"

She responded, "I loved it. Princess Lillianna and the Queen and King always treated me like family. My parents reminded me of the Queen and King a whole lot. My parents were always in love even though there were hard times."

Zalem asked Isabelle about her hard times. She told Zalem that her life was a long story and they would save that story for a more appropriate occasion. Zalem asked Isabelle,

"You promise to tell me the story soon?"
She agreed and said, "When the time is
right." Isabelle paused and said, "Doesn't
someone have training in the morning?"
He responded, "I almost forgot all about
that." He got up quickly and helped her up
as well. He asked, "Can I walk you to your
chambers?"
She replied, "I will be OK, but thank you for
asking. Goodnight," and walked away to go
and check on her mother and head to bed.
Zalem, with his guards guiding him, went
back to his chambers as well.

      The next day as Zalem was getting
ready to train, Lillianna headed off in a horse
and carriage with Zion by her side. They
were headed to the family vacation spot on
an island that King Joseph owned, called
Nathan Island. It was named after King
Joseph's father and was a gift from his
father on his first wedding day.
Zalem walked into the library, where his
instructor was to teach him the ways of
royalty and family history. The instructor
introduced himself to Zalem. He told him,

"My name is Sir Nicholas," and he bowed. He pulled out Zalem's chair and let him sit, then pushed it in. Sir Nicholas ran over to the other side of the table and then sat down. "We are going to first learn about etiquette; when to stand, when to sit, how to address the public, even when to say 'please' and 'thank you.' Later you'll learn to ride a horse, to swim, and to do many more things," said Sir Nicholas.

It was basic stuff, but as each day went by Zalem grew tired of it. One day he learned dining room etiquette, and then he learned how to defend himself better with a sword and shield. He learned to ride a horse. While all of this was going on the King was secretly watching over his son, worried about him.

At this time two weeks had passed, and Zion and Lillianna had returned from their vacation. Lillianna was so excited to see her family. She was even more excited to help Zalem find a queen. The hardest thing for Zalem was to choose a wife. He wanted a woman who he loved, but who would truly help him run the kingdom. The King,

Lathem, Sir Nicholas, Zalem, and Zion all sat in the King's relaxation room, where they looked over many books with different choices for a potential bride.

"Maybe this one," said Zion, as he showed Zalem the book and pointed out, "she looks pretty and loves horseback riding."

Zalem shook his head no and replied, "She is beautiful but has no teeth." The King and Lathem silently laughed.

Then Sir Nicholas pointed out another girl. "She is a duchess and loves reading and going out to travel." Zalem said no because he wanted a wife that would actually run the kingdom and wouldn't be gone all the time. Then Princess Lillianna, Queen Tianna, and Isabelle walked in. "How's the wife search going?" asked Queen Tianna.

"Not well," replied Lathem.

"That's not good, but I had Isabelle whip you guys up a snack." All the guys took the food and said thank you to Isabelle. The King decided to get some fresh air and asked Zalem to go with him. Zalem agreed, and they went for a walk.

"It's a wonderful night, isn't it?" asked the King.

Zalem answered, "Yeah," and looked down at the flowers.

"I know this is hard for you, my son. I had to do the same as you are doing now," said the King.

Zalem looked up at his father and asked him, "How did you choose my mother?"

The King sighed and then sat down by the big fountain. "I knew this question would come from you soon," said the King. He then paused and began again. "Sit down my, son."

Zalem sat down next to his father quietly, giving his undivided attention. The King then began his story. "My father put me in the same predicament that you are in now. I hated doing it, but I had no choice. My father, King Nathan, was a lot pushier than I am. And he wanted to choose a bride for me. I begged my mother to get my father to reconsider choosing my bride. He wouldn't hear it, and then he brought me to your mother, Princess Eliza. My father made a plan to join his kingdom with their kingdom so that their kingdom wouldn't fall apart because they were bankrupt. She was sixteen and I was eighteen, and I did not want anything to do with Eliza or their kingdom.

"My father never listened to me, but my mother always listened to me. So I decided to go to my mother, and she brought it to my attention that I was doing the same thing to Eliza that my father did to me, which was not listening. So the next day I went to meet Princess Eliza at her family kingdom.

The kingdom was so beautiful. While I was walking into the palace to the main hall, I got to see all of their family portraits and precious family heirlooms. In the main hall, King Edward, Queen Liza, and Princess Eliza awaited. When I walked in, my parents were right behind me. They greeted us, but they weren't expecting us to come. Eliza's family was excited to see us come all the way to their kingdom. Then King Edward invited us in for lunch, and I asked him if I could just talk to Eliza before we went off to lunch. All of our parents headed off to the dining hall, and we stayed in the main hall to talk.

"As soon as they left, I asked her how she felt about getting married to a complete stranger. She said that she was nervous and didn't want to get married to me, but then she went down to the village to see the villagers. She began to explain to me that the villagers were poor, and that she and I getting married would help them to have more exports and jobs and money. That was when I really began to understand your mother. She was very passionate about being queen and taking care of her kingdom.

"A year later we married and we were both very happy. So were our parents, and the kingdoms worked well together. Then, the following year, she passed away after giving birth to you. She was eighteen and I was twenty." The King shed a few tears, and Zalem gave him a hug and he told him that he loved him.

Zalem now felt a lot better because he was at least able to choose a wife, while his father wasn't. "I am so grateful to even have a son," said the King.

They both got up and began to head in, and
Zalem asked, "So how did you end up with
Tianna?"

The King replied, "That's a story for another
time, but know that when your mother
passed, I never wanted to marry again."

Zalem walked away happy and eager to hear
how Tianna and his father met and then had
Lillianna.

As they went back to the King's relaxation
room, the King told his son that he was so
glad to spend life with him. "Every time I
look at you, I see your mother, especially
your eyes. I truly miss her; you have no
idea," said the King. They walked back into
the room and began the search to find
Zalem's wife again.

Chapter 5

Early the next morning, Lillianna was worried about her brother as she spoke to Zion and cuddled with Royal. Zion could always tell when Lillianna was worried. Zion explained to Lillianna that love is hard to find and even to stay married. If Zalem had never come back to the kingdom, then Lillianna would be the one trying to find a husband to become king and they might not have been married.

Lillianna agreed and then had a brilliant idea for a way to help Zalem find a wife. Lillianna quickly went, in her night garments, to Zalem to tell him her amazing idea. Lillianna ran into Zalem's chambers, where he still was sleeping. She opened the blinds to let the sunshine in and woke Zalem. Zalem wasn't too excited about being woken up early in the morning." replied Lillianna as she shook him.

"Can't it wait till later?" asked Zalem as he rolled over. He sounded very groggy.

"No, listen," said Lillianna as she rolled him back over.

Zalem wiped his eyes and said, "OK, let's make a deal...." He sat up and continued, "You tell me your idea, and then can I go back to sleep? I have training in a few hours."

Lillianna replied, "All right, I promise..." as she adjusted herself to sit on the bed comfortably. Then she began again, "You ready? Here's my idea."

Zalem replied, "Anytime you're ready," as Lillianna rolled her eyes and continued. "Anyway...let's throw you a royal ball, and you choose three girls from the royal ball to get to know better." She paused and waited for a response and then she asked, "Well, what do you think?"

Zalem responded, "I don't know, Lillianna. I am already nervous about getting married, or even dating one woman. To be in a ballroom with thousands of women is even worse. Then I have to choose three women to date, all at once."

Lillianna responded, "Don't worry. I'll be by your side the entire time."

Zalem easily agreed to do it because he wanted to make Lillianna happy. Lillianna gave her brother a kiss on the forehead and said to him, "You won't regret it. I am going to begin to prepare for the royal ball." As Zalem watched Lillianna walk out, she was very overjoyed.

Zalem rolled out of his giant bed and went to look out the window. He looked at the servants out in the courtyard cleaning. He was very nervous about dealing with this ball. Zalem decided to forget about it and got dressed early before his training. He went to sit by the lake, where he remembered getting to know Lillianna. When he got there, he began to skip rocks in the water. Zalem pulled a portrait of his mother out of his pocket. He wondered what life would have been like if his mother was still alive. Then he heard some crunching footsteps through the grass and heard a voice.

"She was beautiful, wasn't she?" said Queen Tianna.

"Yeah," answered Zalem, as he shoved the portrait back in his pocket.

"Sir Nicholas has been looking for you to begin your training for the day," said the Queen.

Zalem got up and began to make his way inside and then suddenly stopped. He realized that his relationship with Queen Tianna wasn't that strong. It was more awkward than anything, so he turned around and decided to ask her a question.

"Queen Tianna," Zalem loudly called.

She answered, "Yes, Zalem?" She turned toward him and took her attention off the lake.

He then asked, "How did you and my father meet?"

She responded, "I thought Joseph would

have probably told you by now." Zalem shook his head no. Queen Tianna told Zalem to finish his training and then meet her in the main hall, where she would be waiting for him, so they could get a chance to talk about it. Zalem agreed and ran off to do his training.

Nicholas planned to teach Zalem to use a bow and arrow. Then later he gave him swimming lessons. By the end of the day, Zalem was so tired and just wanted to go to bed. But he went to bathe, and then he met with Queen Tianna in the main hall after dinner.

"Sit next to me," said the Queen. There were four chairs in the main hall, for Zalem, the King, the Queen, and Lillianna. The chair Queen Tianna wanted him to sit in was his father's chair. Zalem went and sat there, and Queen Tianna said, "You should get used to sitting there. One day that will be your chair." Prince Zalem smiled. The Queen grinned back and continued, "OK, get ready because it's sort of a long story."

Before the Queen could even begin the story,

they were interrupted. The King came in with a surprise for Zalem. "You look really good in that chair," said the King. Zalem smiled again as he got up from his father's chair. He was sad he couldn't hear the story, but more interested in what his father had to say. The King brought two very special people for him too meet. "Remember the other day when we were talking about your mother and the other palace and her parents?" said the King.

Zalem answered, "Yes, Father."

The King responded, "Well, meet King Edward and Queen Liza...Your grandparents."

Queen Liza began to cry as soon as she saw him. King Edward was so happy to even know he had a grandchild. "You look so much like your mother," said King Edward as he gave him a huge bear hug and began to cry as well. Queen Liza grabbed his face and pulled it down toward her, and she gave him about ten kisses all over his face. Then, she grabbed him around his waist. She wasn't the tallest woman, and Zalem was pretty tall, just like his father. Zalem was so happy that he began to cry as well. They all went to the foyer to get a chance to catch up. Isabelle and Rose got them some food, and they talked all night. They had an amazing time, and Zalem was so excited. Zalem was starting to truly feel like he had a family. He knew his grandparents would help him discover who he was, so he could become king.

The next day, Zalem awoke to Lillianna by his bedside again, though this time she waited for him to wake up. She told him to get up and go to his bath chambers and then meet her outside in the front of the palace so they could go for a walk. Zalem slowly got up. Lillianna rushed him into his bath chambers, so he decided to pick up some speed and got ready a lot faster. He walked through the kitchen and grabbed two crumpets on the way outside. He finished one and began his second one when he got outside. When Lillianna met him outside she grabbed the rest of the crumpet and thanked him for the snack.

"Why did you call me out here?" asked Zalem.

"It's a surprise...Let's just keep walking...so let's talk," said Lillianna.

"What about, Lillianna?" Zalem asked.

"Why don't we talk about your training?" Lillianna suggested.

Zalem sighed and replied, "It's going well, but I wish everything could be a lot easier to learn. Now I am really nervous about my survival test."

Lillianna looked puzzled and asked, "How does that work?"

Zalem replied, "Sir Nicholas wants me to go out to the woods with five guards. We have to find or pick our food, make our own fire, and sleep in the woods. Then the next day I have to lead all five guards back to the castle."

Lillianna replied, "Wow, that must be hard. I would be nervous if I had to do that. You know it's the people in the woods that are scary. The animals aren't even as bad as the people."

Zalem replied, "Yeah, I know, my so-called

mother used to warn me about the forest. I am surprised Zion didn't tell you about it."

Lillianna responded, "Why would he know anything about this? Oh, because he has to choose the five guards?"

Zalem answered, "No, because he *is* one of the five guards."

Lillianna was shocked, because Zion never mentioned that he would be going out to the woods with Zalem. The woods were one of the most unsafe places, because of the people that resided there.

She now wondered why he hadn't told her about this. "This has been decided for a little while, Lill," said Zalem.

As they walked further, they reached the courtyard where Zalem's grandparents were waiting for him. "Hello, love. Did you sleep well?" asked his grandmother.

"I guess so; we were up late last night," responded Zalem.

"Well, come and sit down, my boy. We have so much to discuss," said his grandfather.

Lillianna led him to sit down, and she went to sit down near his grandmother.

"I didn't know we had more to discuss after last night. I thought we would wake up hoarse today," said Zalem as they all laughed.

"I invited everyone here today to discuss this ball and finding Zalem a bride," said Lillianna.

"Oh no, not this again," said Zalem. He was about to get up, and his grandfather sat him down.

"Well, I think it's a great idea," said his Grandmother.

"I am so happy that you even thought we were special enough to be included," said his grandfather.

"Of course you are. Besides King Joseph and Lillianna, I don't have many blood relatives that I know, and I don't trust Uncle Lathem much. My mother is a person I never got to know. Now seeing the both of you makes me feel like a piece of me that died has come back," said Zalem.

"I am glad that you think so highly of us. I have an idea. Edward..." said his grandmother.

"Yes, dear," replied his grandfather.

"Why don't you tell Zalem the story of how we met?" said his Grandmother.

"Yeah, that's a great idea. Maybe that will help you," said Lillianna.

"OK, then, it's story time…We were young, about eighteen, so you're a little late with this whole marriage thing. They usually want us married by nineteen. My father and mother didn't have all their rules like everyone else had. I got to choose who I wanted to marry. I met your grandmother at one of Liza's royal balls that her father used to throw. Liza always hung out with all her friends. That made me very nervous to ask her to dance. Of course Liza was a princess and I was a duke whose kingdom didn't have much money. Liza was the princess that was going to take over the kingdom, so how dare I ask her to dance? There were other princes and dukes there that had money, and they were all flocking around her. I got the title "Duke" when I helped out the Madoness Kingdom. I didn't do as much as these other men had done to earn the name Duke.

Finally, she walked away from her friends to the bath chambers and when she walked out, I grabbed her and asked her to dance. Her father immediately loved me, but her mother was a lot tougher to crack. It took her a long time to approve of me. Liza only had two younger sisters, and they thought I was handsome. I wasn't born a king, but we ran the kingdom with the best justice that we could...We loved the kingdom and our people," said Grandfather.

"That helped as well, by hearing that now I know I have many options. Even though you weren't born royal and had some hardships, you made it work. You weren't destined by your peers, but you made it happen. I could make it work even though I didn't grow up in the royal life and all," said Zalem.

"Now are you ready to let me plan the ball?" asked Lillianna.

"Yes I am," answered Zalem.

"Well, good, but there's not much for you to tell me. I planned most of it. I want this to still be a surprise for the most part, but I just need simple things like food and color

choices. You OK with that?" asked Lillianna.
"I guess I am going to have to be, but I really want to say thank you, Lillianna. You truly care so much about me. I don't know what I'd do without you," said Zalem.
"I was talking to Zion the other day, and he helped me to realize that if you had never come along I would be the one doing this. You know, having to find a husband. So I think I owe it to you, because I don't know what I would do if I had to go through this," said Lillianna. They smiled at each other and gave each other a hug. Then the servants brought out some food for them to eat and they had a beautiful lunch.

Chapter 6

Before they knew it, the ball was upon them.
Lillianna decided to surprise Zalem and
throw him his royal ball on his twentieth
birthday. Lillianna designed the ballroom so
beautifully. Even the aroma was appealing.
The first thing that could be seen upon
walking in was a huge, but gorgeous,
dazzling chandelier. Then there were brilliant
red drapes, because red was Zalem's favorite
color. The drapes were held open by solid
gold drape holders mounted on the wall.
There were huge round tables that each held
at least twenty people. Each table was fitted
with a silky eggshell tablecloth, lined with
gold. The tables were decorated with fresh-

cut rose petals out of the garden. There were also custom-made red crown candles encrusted with diamonds. The candles were imported from his grandparents' kingdom of Viel. In the center of each table sat an arrangement of assorted red and white roses.

The Kingdom looked amazing, and the guests were definitely enjoying themselves with the band that was playing. Uncle Lathem had picked the band after he heard them playing in town. He loved it, so he invited them to play at the ball. As each person came to the ball, their arrival was announced.

When Zalem arrived at the ball, trumpets were blown and the guards were lined up along each side of the stairs, facing one another. They were lined up not only along the stairs, but also part of the red carpet. The guards' swords were pulled and raised to the ceiling. The guards then crossed their swords together to make an arch for Zalem to walk through. When he was done, he was greeted by all of the guests. Zalem was very nervous, but a little excited as well about his birthday. If it was left up to Zalem, he would not be having this ball.

As soon as Zalem began to walk toward Lillianna, at least fifteen women ran toward him and began to converse with him. Zalem didn't really know what to say to the women, but he began to answer their questions and do a little small talk. Isabelle realized that Zalem seemed nervous as she was pouring drinks.

"Lillianna, Zalem looks a little uncomfortable. Wouldn't you say so? He has been talking to them for about forty-five minutes, and it still looks strange," said Isabelle.

"Yes, I do agree," said Lillianna as she sipped her drink. She began to speak again. "Why don't you excuse him from those women?" She winked and laughed.

Isabelle laughed as well, and she answered, "Yes, my lady." She took off her apron and walked toward him, shyly smiling. "Prince Zalem," said Isabelle, as she bowed.

Zalem replied, "Yes Isabelle?" The women

were shocked to see him use her name, because servants were unimportant in their kingdoms.

"The royal family, especially Lillianna, wishes to speak to you," said Isabelle.

"You heard the lady. I'll be back later," said Zalem, as the women tugged on his hands and clothes sadly as he left. But one got to pinch his butt, and she smiled and waved. Zalem turned red as he walked away with Isabelle. He spoke softly to her. "Thank you so much for getting me away from those crazy women."

Isabelle laughed and responded, "Anything for you...my Prince."

"You know, you can call me Zalem," he said.

"Yes, I do know, but I'd rather not. I am still a servant," said Isabelle, as they reached the thrones where his family was sitting. Zalem sat next to Lillianna on his right, their father to his left, and Queen Tianna next to King Joseph.

"So how are you enjoying your ball?" Tianna asked.

"It's all great, thanks to Lillianna," said

Zalem. Even though Zalem wasn't too happy with this whole ball thing, he didn't want to let Lillianna down.

"You're welcome, Zalem. I just want you to find love," said Lillianna.

Isabelle came back to pour Zalem a drink, as he looked at her and asked her to dance. "I have so much work, and I am not really even supposed to," said Isabelle nervously.

"Are you not doing as a prince asked you to do?" said King Joseph, smiling.

Zalem smiled and stretched out his hand toward hers. She smiled and then joined him. They got onto the dance floor and began to dance, but started a conversation as well. "You look very beautiful, Isabelle," said Zalem.

"Thank you, Prince Zalem," said Isabelle.

"Please stop calling me that when we are together or alone, just call me Zalem, OK?" he asked.

Isabelle responded, "Ok...Zalem; that feels so weird." As they danced, they got a lot of evil eyes from many of the women across the dance floor. Zalem and Isabelle were laughing together as a woman named Abigail interrupted them and asked to steal Zalem away. Isabelle agreed, and responded, "I have a lot of work to do anyway."

Isabelle walked away. Abigail joined hands with Zalem, and they began to dance. "Let me introduce myself. My name is Abigail; I am eighteen. Everyone knows your name; it's Prince Zalem. So you don't have to introduce yourself," she said.

"It's truly nice to meet you," said Zalem.

"So, you throw an amazing ball," said Abigail.

"No, it wasn't me; it was my sister. She did all of this. She's good at all this stuff," said Zalem. They got silent for a bit and then Zalem spoke. "Well, I should be getting to meet some of the other guests."

Abigail responded, "It was really nice that I got a chance to dance with you. Thank you!"

Zalem looked at her and said, "You're welcome."

As he began to walk away, another woman grabbed him and said, "Hello, Prince Zalem, my name is Evangeline, from the Madoness

Kingdom. I am twenty years old. You're even more gorgeous close up," she said as she curtsied. He bowed back to her and said hello. "Can I take you outside for a quick walk?" asked Evangeline.

He looked at Lillianna and then looked at Evangeline and replied, "Sure, we can go for a walk."

They walked through the palace in silence. Then Evangeline decided to break the ice and said, "This is a beautiful palace." She looked at some portraits on the wall.

"So where are you from again?" asked Zalem. She replied, "I am a duchess from the Kingdom of Madoness. It was the longest trip I have ever been on."

Zalem thanked her for coming all the way to meet him and then asked, "May I ask how you were given the title duchess?"

She responded, "I know I don't look like much of a warrior, but I fought and saved the King of Madoness and his family from a great evil."

Zalem wanted to hear more, but he realized that it was getting late. "We better start walking back. Dinner should be served soon and they are probably looking for me by now," said Zalem.

"Well, let me at least say happy birthday to you," said Evangeline. He was about to thank her, when she pushed him against the wall and gave him a long, passionate kiss. Her body was pressed against him, and he loved every minute of it. "I wanted to give you a present and to let you know that I am really interested in getting to know you better," said Evangeline as she lowered her leg off of his right side. Zalem smiled and watched her walk away. He loved the way she walked. He then walked back to the ballroom and was eager to meet more women.

Then one of the guards announced that dinner was about to be served, and everyone should be seated. All the tables were round except for the Royal table. Their table was rectangular, and they all sat on one side of the table, facing the crowd. From left to right they sat in this order: first Zion, then Lillianna, then Queen Tianna, King Joseph, and Zalem. There were two seats next to him that were empty, and he wondered why. The last person to the right at the end of the table was his Uncle Lathem. The guards announced that there was a surprise for Prince Zalem, and everyone should look forward.

In came his grandparents, who made an announcement. "Zalem, happy birthday. We are truly excited to be here today for you," said his grandfather.

"Yes, darling, we are, and happy birthday from me as well. And now, here is your surprise," said his grandmother. Then they both took their seats. His grandmother sat next to Zalem, and his grandfather sat next to her. There was a puff of smoke and out came a ringleader with acrobats, lions, a man that juggled fire, and much more. Zalem was so excited and loved his present. While the circus was going on, they served dinner. During dinner, the circus continued to entertain. "How is your evening going, Zalem?" asked his father.

"It's actually going amazing, and this time I

am not lying," said Zalem as they both laughed. His grandmother overheard them laughing, and she told King Joseph to give Zalem his gift.

"Oh yes, I almost forgot," said the King.

"What could it be?" said Zalem.

"Don't worry, honey, you'll love it," said his grandmother.

Zalem watched as his father began to explain and pulled a box out of his pocket.

"It was your mother's," said the King.

His grandmother continued to explain, "Well, let me explain a little more. It was a ring my father gave me, and I loved it so much that I saved it for Eliza and then gave it to King Joseph as a wedding ring for your mother."

King Joseph continued and said, "Since your mother passed, I have had it in my possession with some of your keepsakes this entire time, and now it seems like a fitting time to give it to you." He then opened the box and showed Zalem.

"Wow, dad, that's big of you to give me that ring," said Zalem.

"Yeah, I guess it is, but this ring is here now

so you could hopefully get a chance to give it to your bride-to-be. I really want you to find love like your grandparents, or even as your mother and I, or your step mother and I. Even though it feels like love, you can be blinded by other things, and it could make you choose the wrong person," said King Joseph.

Zalem thanked them both and promised to treasure this ring with all his heart.

"I know you don't have your mom but I am here for you, baby," said his grandmother as she gave him a kiss on the forehead.

After dinner, his stepmother had beautiful desserts for Zalem. There was a huge cake designed as a giant sword. They had little dessert roses in different colors, such as white and red, made of milk chocolate and white chocolate. The guests enjoyed the desserts as well. After dessert, they all rose again to dance, but by that time Queen Tianna, King Joseph, and Zalem's grandparents had grown tired. They retired for the night, but not before wishing Zalem the best of luck.

As the ball continued, Zalem met a lot of women and decided to ask one to dance. He whispered in her ear, "I was brought to you by your beauty," and she giggled in a very annoying laugh.

"What's your name?" asked Zalem.

"My name is Alexandra, and I am from the kingdom of Viel," she answered.

"How extraordinary that you are from my grandparents' kingdom," Zalem said. Alexandra was very nervous and began to step on Zalem's feet. Zalem grew tired of being stepped on and made an excuse to leave. While he walked away, he thought, *that's the last time I ask a woman to dance.* Zalem began to walk slowly and another woman approached him.

"Happy birthday, Prince Zalem," she said, as she curtsied to him. Zalem turned and looked at her and smiled. She was stunning. He bowed back and said thank you. He kissed her hand, and then they both gazed at one another. She almost tripped and snapped back to reality as she said, "How rude of me not to introduce myself. My name is Cassandra, from the Cruze family."

She looked so confident with her nose in the air, but Zalem wasn't really too familiar with the Cruze family. "I am sorry my lady, I have heard of your name, but I don't really know the background of your family," said Zalem as he took a drink from one of the servants and drank some.

She did the same as him and drank as well and began to explain her family. "Well, that is a surprise, because everyone usually knows my family, and always expects handouts from us. My family does a lot of business with this kingdom. My family makes and trades cotton. We even make a lot of the clothing your family wears. We are one of the biggest in exports to other kingdoms," said Cassandra.

"Wow, that's amazing. I would love to go and see how our clothing is made," said Zalem.

"Really?" Cassandra responded in a dull voice. Then she took a sip of her drink and responded in a happier voice, "Well, then, that's great. I'll set up a date and let you know."

He asked, "How old are you?"

She responded, "Seventeen."

Lillianna and Zion decided that they were going to retire for the night, and when Zalem saw them leave, he decided to call it a night as well. He wished Cassandra a good night and on his way out. He saw that Lathem was still on the dance floor, having fun. He smiled, and as he continued walking out, Zalem ran into another woman. "Goodnight, Prince Zalem," said the woman.

"Goodnight...well, I don't know your name, so how am I supposed to say goodnight?" said Zalem, smiling the entire time.

"My name is Veronica and thank you for asking," she said. "You look so tired, Prince Zalem. Do you want me to walk you to your chambers?"

Zalem agreed, and they began to walk and talk. "So where are you from, Veronica?" asked Zalem.

She answered, "I am from the kingdom of Euselus. I am actually Princess Veronica. My father is King Maxwell."

"I don't know why I didn't recognize you

before. I saw you at Lillianna's wedding. You look just like your father," said Zalem.

"Yes, everyone says that; especially my mother used to," said Veronica as she looked down at her bracelet. Then she began to twirl her bracelet. Zalem noticed that she began to look very sad, so he rested his hands on hers.

Veronica began to cry, and Zalem began to speak. "I know it's hard that she passed away. I know the feeling."

Veronica smiled and looked up at him, and then she gave him a hug and apologized to him. "I am so selfish for even bringing that up, knowing the story of you and your mother. I am sorry," she said as she turned away.

Zalem turned her around and dried her tears. "Look at the bright side, Veronica. You at least knew your mother and got to grow up knowing the royal ways. I didn't have my mother or a family. Just be grateful for the memories that you have," said Zalem. As he held her hand and they began to walk again. "Well, these are my chambers," said Zalem.

"I truly enjoyed our conversation," said Veronica.

Zalem had an idea. "Wait here by the door while I speak to one of my guards," said Zalem. Veronica agreed, and Zalem went and found his guard Sir Luther. Zalem called him Sir Luther because he was much older than Zalem and he never felt right calling him Luther. "Sir Luther, can you please do me a favor and get some servants together? I need three guest chambers ready for three guests, please. I also want an announcement of the three women I have chosen to stay here. I would like to ask Lady Cassandra of the Cruze family and Duchess Evangeline of the Madoness Kingdom to be invited as guests. If they have already left, then please send for them in the morning," said Zalem.

"Yes Sire, but what if they ask why?" said Sir Luther.

Zalem responded, "Let it be a surprise, but please send a servant to my chamber doors to take one of the women to her guest chambers." Zalem thanked Sir Luther and went back to his chambers, looking for

Veronica. When he returned, Veronica was pacing the floor. "Relax, my lady. I was just getting one of my servants to help me," said Zalem, as one of the servants rapidly approached them.

"Yes, my Prince," the servant answered as she bowed.

"Thank you for coming," said Zalem to the servant. "Veronica, I wish for you to spend a night, or a few nights, in the palace so I could get to know you better," said Zalem. Princess Veronica looked nervous and in shock, but she was so excited. "Well...OK, I guess," she said.

Zalem responded, "Great, well then this servant..." Zalem paused, because he hated calling her "servant." "What is your name?" Zalem asked the servant.

"Rebecca," she answered as she smiled and blushed because she was so honored that Zalem asked her for her name.

"That's a beautiful name," said Zalem.

"Thank you, Sire," said Rebecca, as she bowed again.

"Now, Rebecca, can you please take Veronica

to wash up and then to her chambers?"
asked Zalem.

"Yes, Sire," answered Rebecca. Zalem and
Veronica glanced at each other as Rebecca
spoke. "Goodnight, Sire."

He replied back, "Goodnight, Rebecca."

Rebecca said, "This way, my lady."

Zalem walked into his chambers, waving to
Veronica as she glanced back at him. He
shut his door and stood behind it thinking
about his amazing night. Zalem was excited
about finding his bride. He went to sleep
that night with a smile on his face.

Chapter 7

The next day Zalem awoke to Lillianna by his bedside. "You never fail, do you?" asked Zalem.

"Well, that's rude, after I worked so hard to give you an amazing royal ball. That you enjoyed, I saw," said Lillianna in a taunting voice. Zalem smiled at Lillianna, and she continued, "I know you lied to me in the beginning of the ball when you said you were enjoying yourself. By the end, you were smiling and dancing," said Lillianna.

"Yeah, I really did, after Evangeline kissed me in the foyer," said Zalem.

"Wow, she moves fast. I can't believe she

kissed you," said Lillianna as she became over excited.

"Yeah, and I invited three women to stay at the palace, so I could get to know them better," said Zalem.

"That must be exciting. I hope you did not choose that Alexandra girl," said Lillianna as they both laughed. "You two would never get through your first dance at your wedding," said Lillianna.

Zalem replied, "Abigail wasn't any better. It felt so awkward."

Lillianna replied, "Well, who did you pick?"

Zalem responded, "I chose Cassandra Cruze, and..."

Lillianna interrupted, "Wait, do you mean from the Cruze family that makes our clothing?"

Zalem replied, "Yeah, her. Why?"

Lillianna responded, "She seemed very shallow to me my entire life. I don't know what you see in her, but good luck. Forget about what I said; just tell me who else you picked."

Zalem replied, "OK, Duchess Evangeline

from the Madoness Kingdom, and Princess Veronica. I didn't get Princess Veronica's age. How old is she?"

Lillianna replied, "She is twenty-one."

Zalem responded, "Oh, she's older than me."

Lillianna responded after a pause, "OK, then, I am happy for you. You finally got your three women."

Zalem then said, "I am actually very excited about getting to know them."

Lillianna replied, "Well, don't you want to get ready to see them, then?"

Zalem responded, "I can't right now; I have training to do. After my training I want to have dinner with them."

Lillianna replied, "OK, I will make sure everything is put together for dinner."

Zalem then said, "Thank you."

Lillianna replied, "Don't mention it. Now get out of bed, Mr. Lazy."

Zalem replied, "I am far from lazy," as they both laughed. Zalem got out of bed and went to his bath chambers. Lillianna got up and decided to head down to get the women outside to watch Zalem train. Then she headed to the kitchen to prepare the dinner menu.

When Zalem finally got ready, he walked through the kitchen to grab a snack. Then he went outside to work on his defense skills. Sir Nicholas had a lot of booby traps and tricks set up so that Zalem could train in the courtyard. While Zalem was training as, the three women watched.

"Doesn't he look amazing?" said Cassandra.

"Yes he does; he is so strong," said Evangeline.

"Why are you so quiet, Veronica?" asked Cassandra.

"Just a little nervous," said Veronica.

"You should be nervous. I am going to make sure that nothing gets in the way of me getting closer to Zalem," said Evangeline.

Cassandra rolled her eyes and turned away.

"Whatever you say, Evangeline," said Cassandra.

"What's that supposed to mean?" said Evangeline.

"All I am going to say is that you lack class, and if he really falls for you, he has no taste in women," said Cassandra.

Veronica laughed silently. "Well, that's rude, Cassandra. You're not that special. You're not even royalty, so I don't know what makes you any better. You're not even worthy," said Evangeline.

"Now, children, as good as this may make the two of you feel, can the both of you just stop and grow up for a few minutes? I don't know what makes either of you think you are worthy. You both have awful personalities. I am the only princess. I am the only one entitled to anything, but I am not perfect, either. So if you are done, please, for two seconds...Ladies, just SHUT IT," said Veronica.

Both women were in shock, and each of them grabbed their fans and began to fan themselves. Veronica glanced at Zalem and wondered what life would be like with him. Then she decided she wasn't worthy of him. Veronica never thought highly of herself, but by seeing these two women, she quickly figured out how selfish they were and she knew she had to protect Zalem from them.

Lillianna looked down from the dining room outside at the courtyard at the women and then at Zalem. "I know it was my idea for Zalem to date these women, but now I am thinking this is a bad idea," said Lillianna.

"I am worried, too, but Zalem is a big boy. He'll make the right decision," said Queen Tianna.

"Rose, can you see if we have red wine in the cellar?" asked Lillianna.

"Yes, my lady," answered Rose, as she bowed and left the room.

"Isabelle, can you please help me to prepare a menu for dinner? Let's go down to the kitchen," said Queen Tianna. Lillianna got up from the windowsill that had a window seat, and Zion walked in. "Be back later, baby," said Queen Tianna as she walked out. "Hello, Zion," said Queen Tianna as she continued to walk.

He answered, "My lady," and did a slight bow. He said, "Hello, how are you?" as he gave Lillianna a kiss.

"I am great. Just trying to help Zalem get dinner together," said Lillianna.

"I love you," said Zion, and he gave her a hug from behind.

"I love you, too. Zion, can I ask you a question?" said Lillianna.

"Yes, my love, anything," said Zion as Lillianna turned around and looked him in the eyes.

"Why didn't you tell me about your trip to the forest?" asked Lillianna.

"How did you find out about that?" asked Zion.

"Zalem told me and don't try to answer my question with a question. Now can you look at me and answer?" asked Lillianna as she caressed his face with her hands.

"Lillianna, I was worried about you knowing about that because I know you're pregnant," said Zion.

Lillianna looked at him in shock and asked him, "How did you know?" Zion said, "I overheard you with Isabelle when you were in the foyer." He looked disappointed.

"Oh, Zion, that was wrong of you to keep a secret from me when I kept one from you," said Lillianna.

"Yes, that would be, but that's not what I was doing," said Zion.

"Now you want to lie to me. Did you ever hear why I didn't tell anyone?" said Lillianna as she began to walk away.

Zion grabbed Lillianna and lightly shook her. "Relax, Lillianna, I know why. Stop and let me speak. I am excited about the baby, but I was just trying to stop you from worrying. All I am is a concerned father-to-be and a husband. I don't want you to be stressed."

Lillianna smiled and began to laugh because she felt ridiculous. "I want to be a dad, especially because I did not grow up with my dad. I vaguely remember him being there, and when he died it felt like nothing because I never knew him," said Zion. They kissed, and Zion guided Lillianna to sit by the windowsill with him so they could talk some more. "You should get more used to relaxing. This is how you are going to be for a while," said Zion.

"Yeah, I know," said Lillianna.

"If it truly upsets you, I won't go," said Zion.

"No, it's OK. Zalem really needs you," said

Lillianna.

"But you need me, as well," said Zion.

"That is true, but I want you to do this. I am going to tell the family soon about the pregnancy. Will you do it with me?" asked Lillianna.

"Yes, sure, as long as you promise to rest and relax and tell me next time if you have news," said Zion.

"Yes, I will, I promise. But I want to announce this to the family before you leave," said Lillianna.

"That makes sense. Sorry it ruins your plans," said Zion.

"It doesn't ruin my plans. I was going to tell everyone at the next town meeting, which is two weeks away," said Lillianna.

"You sure this won't bother you?" said Zion.

"No, it won't bother me. Just be by my side when I tell the family, OK?" asked Lillianna. Zion nodded his head, and they both agreed to tell them the next day at tea. There would be a message sent to the town board as well.

Later that evening, dinner was served. The three women Zalem invited were dressed and prepared for dinner. King Joseph sat at the head of the table, and to his right sat Zalem, Cassandra, then Evangeline and Veronica. To the King's left sat Queen Tianna, then Lillianna, Zion, and Lathem. Zalem's grandparents were at their kingdom. King Joseph began the conversation. "How is the training going?"

Zalem answered him, "It is OK. I am having a hard time because I am so nervous about the whole forest trip."

"Why is it bothering you so much, Zalem?" asked Queen Tianna.

"Because I would rather do it and get it over with," said Zalem.

"Then why don't you just move forward with it, to get it done early?" asked Lathem.

"That's a great idea," said Veronica.

"Yeah, it would be easier to get it off my mind," said Zalem.

"Well, then it's settled. Tomorrow morning, Zion, have your guards ready to begin their journey," said King Joseph.

Lillianna looked at Zion, and he knew that they had to make the announcement. Zion

stood up and said, "I have an announcement
to make. Well, Lillianna and I do. Love...why
don't you tell them?" said Zion, as he held
her hand in comfort.

Then Lillianna stood up as well. "I have
wanted to tell you guys about this for a
while," she said.

"Darling, you can tell us anything. Go on,"
said the Queen.

"I know I can, but let me just say it and then
explain it...I am four months pregnant," said
Lillianna. The King began to choke. Zalem
hit him on the back, and the food came out
of this throat. Zalem handed him a drink.

"Father, are you OK?" asked Lillianna, as her
mother hopped up in excitement.

"Oh my, I am going to be a grandmother. I
could never tell you were pregnant because
you're carrying so well," said the Queen.
Then the Queen began to cry and gave
Lillianna a hug. The King remained silent as
everything was going on.

"I am so excited for the both of you. That's
why you have been so quiet, Lillianna," said
Zalem, as he hugged Lillianna and shook

Zion's hand.

"I will make sure that I guard that child with my life," said Lathem.

Queen Tianna hugged Zion, and she sat everyone down. She wanted to hear Lillianna's explanation. "Why didn't you two tell anyone?" asked the Queen.

"That wasn't my intention, but Zion didn't know anything. He overheard when Isabelle and I discovered that I was. We confronted each other about it earlier today. I had originally planned to tell everyone at the next town meeting. My plans changed when I found out that the two of you were going into the forest. That's what made me realize that I had to do this soon. When Zion and I talked about it, we agreed to tell everyone at tea tomorrow. What made us do it now was that you moved the forest trip up to tomorrow," said Lillianna.

"Zion, Lillianna, once again congrats. I am going to be an uncle, but I am one person who knows how important it is to have both of your parents in your life. If you two are expecting, it doesn't make sense that you go with me into the forest. It could be dangerous," said Zalem.

"Lillianna and I already talked about this, and we decided that it would be best if I went," said Zion.

Then Lillianna turned to her father, who still hadn't said anything. "Daddy, you haven't said anything. Daddy...Daddy," said Lillianna, as she grabbed his arm.

"Sorry, sweetheart...I am excited, but...scared for you as well," said King Joseph. Hearing all of this reminded him once again of when Eliza passed away.

"Daddy, I love you. You know that," said Lillianna. She got up and hugged him.

"Yes, I do, but I do not want anything to happen to you," said the King.

"I agree, but Daddy, I am scared, nervous, and excited as well. I have so many emotions going on, and I need everyone's support," said Lillianna. She gave her father a kiss on the forehead and then went and sat down.

"This child is a big part of our lives, and I want all of you to be there for him or her," said Lillianna.

"Are you exactly four months, darling?" asked the Queen.

"Yes," said Lillianna.

"I know you'll be an amazing mother, Lillianna, and you will be a great father, Zion," said Veronica.

"I wish you all the best," said Cassandra, even though she didn't have much love for children.

"Yes, congrats, darling," said Evangeline.

"Thank you," said Lillianna as their main course arrived.

Later that night, Zalem took Cassandra for a walk. "Remember when I told you I would go and see how clothing is made?" said Zalem.

"Yes, I do," answered Cassandra, as she turned her head and rolled her eyes, wondering why he would even want to go there.

"Well, I go out to the forest tomorrow, and hopefully I should be back in two days. When I return, I want to take you up on that offer," said Zalem.

"That is amazing. I can't wait," said

Cassandra.

While they were talking, Evangeline and Veronica spoke by the pond. "I know that Zalem and I belong together. Two people so perfect—how could it not work?" said Evangeline.

Veronica looked away in disgust. She then turned back and answered Evangeline. "Whatever floats your boat and doesn't sink your ship." She tossed her hair back.

"You are going to stop being so rude, Veronica. Anyway, I am going to interrupt Cassandra and talk to Zalem." Evangeline got up, walked over, and interrupted Cassandra and Zalem.

"Can I steal him away?" said Evangeline. "Sure," said Cassandra, even though in her head she really wanted to slap her. She faked a smile and said, "I am going to retire, goodnight." She gave Zalem a kiss on the cheek and walked away to her chambers. She was very upset.

"So, how are you?" said Evangeline, as she wrapped her arms around his neck.

"I am great; a little tired, but I am OK," said

Zalem as Evangeline gave him a kiss. Meanwhile, Veronica got up and decided to go and talk to Zalem before she went to bed. "We never do much talking when I am with you," said Zalem. "Does it really matter?" said Evangeline, as she kissed him again. Veronica saw them kissing and decided to walk to her chambers. Zalem broke away from a kiss and began to talk to Evangeline, "I want to meet your parents."

Evangeline said, "OK, whatever you want," as she went for another kiss.

Zalem dodged the kiss. "Wait here, let me check on Veronica," said Zalem. He walked away and realized that Veronica was gone and walked back to Evangeline.

"Well, that was quick. What's wrong?" said Evangeline.

"She wasn't there. I wonder where she is," said Zalem.

"Oh, sorry to hear that. I am going to my chambers, and I was wondering if you want to join me there tonight," asked Evangeline.

"I don't know," said Zalem.

"Come on, it would be fun," said Evangeline.

"Maybe, but I have to go and check on my plans for tomorrow," said Zalem.

"OK, I'll be waiting," said Evangeline.

"Let me walk you in, OK?" said Zalem.

Meanwhile, Zion's family had come to visit him. Ethan was walking in the hallway, when he ran into Veronica. "Sorry, my lady," said Ethan. He was shocked by her beauty.

"No, it is my fault," said Veronica. She curtsied and he bowed back.

Ethan began to walk away, and Veronica called, "Sir?"

He answered, "Yes, my lady," as he turned around.

"How do you bump into a lady and not give her your name?" asked Veronica.

He smiled and answered, "Pardon me. My name is Ethan Blackmore. And yours?"

She realized he wasn't royal because of his surname. She replied "My name is Veronica and thank you for asking." She laughed and spoke again. "So what is a gorgeous guy like you doing in the palace?"

He responded, "My brother invited me and my younger brother to spend the night because he had some big news."

Veronica then asked, "Wow! Well, who is your brother?" as she smiled.

"My brother is Prince Zion," said Ethan.

"Oh, it is a great surprise—I already know what it is. Let me say an early congrats," said Veronica.

"You're funny," said Ethan. He began to laugh and responded, "OK, then, I guess I'll say an early thank you. Now, let me ask you what are you doing here?"

Before Veronica could answer, Zalem came around the corner. "Princess Veronica, I looked everywhere for you," said Zalem.

"Wow, you're a princess? I know what that means," said Ethan as he bowed and greeted Zalem, then walked away. He walked around the corner and leaned against the wall, feeling embarrassed.

"I hope I didn't interrupt anything," said Zalem.

"No, you didn't," answered Veronica. Ethan heard her answer and continued down the other hall to see Zion.

"Please let me talk to you before I leave

tomorrow," said Zalem.

"OK, then let's walk and talk," said Veronica.
As they began to walk, a lot of thoughts were running through Veronica's head.

"So, I'll miss you tomorrow," said Zalem.

"Really?" said Veronica with delight and shock.

"Yes. You sound shocked to hear that," said Zalem.

"Well, not to sound strange, but there are two other women here that would miss you as well," said Veronica.

"Yes, you are correct, but you're the only one that didn't look at me like a piece of meat. You actually look at me like a person," said Zalem.

"Well, I wouldn't say that," responded Veronica.

"I would. You're an amazing girl, and I really want to get to know you," said Zalem as he leaned over and gave her a kiss.

Veronica had no intentions of being kissed, or even trying to kiss him. She stepped back and then straight into her chambers, with no words spoken. Zalem didn't know what to say or do, so he walked away to his chambers to get ready for his trip tomorrow. He didn't really understand what had happened. He didn't know what to say or do.

Back in her chambers, Veronica began to cry. Then a faraway voice spoke. "What could you possibly be crying about?" Veronica recognized the voice and answered, "What do you care?"

Then the voice felt even closer, and she began to see a figure in the dark. "You're correct. I don't care, but I need to make sure that your head is on straight," said the voice. "What is wrong with you? Haven't you tortured me enough?" said Veronica.

Then the person approached her and sat down in front of her. "I think you have forgotten our deal."

"I know the deal," said Veronica.

"Well, then let me just refresh your memory. Your father will die if you do not marry Zalem. We will kill Zalem, Joseph, and Lathem and anyone who stands in our way," said the mysterious person.

"Didn't I tell you I know already? Can you

just get away from me? This is not right.
Zalem and his family are great people, so
why do this to them? Even better, let me ask
why even put me in this predicament? Why
not just kill them now?" asked Veronica.

"That is none of your business. Just get
done what I need done," said the mysterious
person.

"Yes, mother," answered Veronica.

"What a good girl," said Veronica's mother,
as she got up and left her chambers, in her
disguise as a servant.

Chapter 8

The next day, everyone woke up nervous to go into the forest. The men were lined up, ready to go. There were five guards: Sir Luther, Sir Francis, Sir Zion, Sir Adam, and Sir Timothy. Two other people were joining them as well, King George and his son, Prince Blake. King George decided to go to watch over his son, and Prince Blake went for his training. They ruled the Balcot Kingdom, which was very good friends with Zaru.

All the men waited for Zalem. As Zalem gathered his gear and was on his way out, Princess Veronica ran out to say good-bye.

She ran up to him as he was walking into the courtyard, and she gave him a kiss. Everyone saw them kiss. Ethan saw the kiss and turned away, and the women were green with envy. She wished him well and told him she would miss him. Zalem was surprised but happy because he really liked Veronica and was shocked the other day with her response to his kiss.

King Joseph wished them well and gave Zalem his sword and shield. Zalem loved the gift, and he gave his old sword and shield to Zion. Zion gave his to Timothy, because he was second in command. They loaded up and headed into the forest. As they walked in, they began to converse.

"I hope this is as easy as it looks," said Zalem to Prince Blake.

"I can't promise you that," said Blake.

"What makes you say that?" asked Zalem.

"I have already done this once before, and it did not turn out well for me," answered Blake.

"Do you mind if I ask you what happened?" asked Zalem.

"I'd rather not explain, but I'll say this: I lost one of my guards. He was my brother, and he was trying to protect me," said Blake. Zalem stopped, then looked at the ground and shook off the news. Then he began to walk again. Zalem thought of Zion first, because he was the closest thing to a brother that he had. Zion had put aside his life to come with him. Zalem realized that he had to watch over Zion. Then Zalem answered, "That's awful. I couldn't even imagine what that feels like. I didn't grow up with any siblings. I met Lillianna later, and I love her a lot." He gazed at the sky.

"Yeah I know. That's why I take this very seriously. My father does as well; that's why he is here to help me through this," said Blake.

"I won't ask you how your brother died, but I want to know: how did this experience change your life?" asked Zalem.

"It changed my life a lot. My mother blames me for his death. My brother was supposed to become king, and I learned through this that you only live once," answered Blake as he began to walk ahead.

Zalem trailed behind and bumped into Zion, who was walking forward. Zion helped him get back on track, and they continued walking.

They finally reached an open path and decided to take a break. Zion decided that while they were resting, he would figure out where they should set up camp for the night. He looked at the map and decided that if they continued walking at the same pace, they would be able to stop at the waterfall. Then they would return the next day to the palace. After about five minutes, they began to walk again.

Before they knew it, it was the end of the day, and they had reached the waterfall. All the men were tired and hungry. Sir Adam and Sir Timothy went to fetch food, and King George and Zalem went to fetch firewood. As Zalem and King George walked away, they began to talk. Zalem felt very intimidated around the King. "So how do you feel, my boy...about becoming king?" King George asked.

"I don't know. I am very nervous about becoming King," said Zalem as he began to look at the ground and kick rocks.

King George put his hand on Zalem's shoulder, and their eyes met. "Hey, don't worry, being king isn't easy, but you'll get to understand it," said King George. At that moment, Zalem began to relax and not feel so intimidated.

"How do you know I am made for this?" said Zalem.

"I know because you remind me a little of myself. I was so nervous about taking the throne that I ran away," said King George.

"You're kidding; you ran away?" said Zalem, as they began to laugh.

"Yeah...I know it's hard to believe, but I ran out of the kingdom, into the town on horseback," said King George.

"So what made you come back?" asked Zalem.

"When I reached the town, I saw the people. They welcomed me in, and I knew from then on that I wanted to protect these people. I did everything for my kingdom. There are certain people that are born to lead," said King George.

"How do you know when you are born to lead?" asked Zalem.

"Believe me, you'll realize it soon," said King George.

Then Zalem heard a noise, and he quickly turned around, dropping the wood. But he saw nothing.

"Did you hear something?" asked King George.

"No, it was the wind," said Zalem as he gathered the wood quickly together. They decided to return to camp with the firewood. Prince Blake and Zalem set the fire. They all gathered around the fire and then Sir Adam and Sir Timothy returned with food. They picked mostly a lot of berries. Zion decided to show them how to catch their dinner. He saw an ox and shot it with an arrow, killed it, then cooked it. Zion always was amazing at archery. They all ate and retired early.

The next day they woke and gathered their camp together. Then they began their journey back to the castle. As they began to walk, everyone noticed that Blake had a huge attitude. Blake bumped into Zalem and screamed at him, "Walk faster, Zalem. I don't know why all of you are walking so slowly." The King shouted, "Blake!"

Then Zalem interrupted King George and said, "Blake, we are all supposed to stick together and look out for one another."

Blake said, "Well, you guys do that, and I'll continue forward, with or without you all," as he walked forward. His father kept calling his name, but he ignored him and kept on walking.

Prince Blake vanished ahead, and Zalem asked, "What's his problem?"

The King answered, "We got into a fight last night, and it got so bad that he told me he wished I would disappear."

Then, all of a sudden, they heard a scream and a loud noise. All swords were drawn as they all ran forward. The men found Prince Blake knocked unconscious and being robbed by thieves. When the three thieves saw everyone coming, they blew a whistle that was made out of wood and many more thieves arrived. All of them realized that they had to fight for their lives.

Zalem fought and wounded many men, but didn't really want to take their lives. All the men watched each other's backs. Zalem especially watched Zion's the most. Zion was fighting a man and another hit him in the leg with an arrow. He couldn't fight back so Zalem and King George protected him. In the middle of the fighting, Prince Blake awoke and saw his father fighting for his life. Blake searched for his sword but couldn't find it because one of the thieves had taken it from him. Blake had to think on his feet so he threw a few rocks at the thieves. The three men saw Blake throwing rocks at them and went after Blake. Blake quickly realized that they were coming to get him, so he ran away from them through the forest.

As the men began to chase Blake, Zalem and King George followed him. Zalem told Sir Francis to protect Zion with his life. Prince Blake ran fast and was looking back, so he did not see the cliff ahead of him. The three men that were chasing Prince Blake ran straight off the cliff as well. They tried grabbing onto anything, even Blake, to get a chance to save themselves, but nothing worked. The three men fell to their deaths. The King ran ahead of Zalem, but when Zalem heard the screams, he tried to grab the King to stop him, but it was too late. King George fell off the cliff as well.

Zalem heard the King's scream and slowly walked through the bushes and saw the cliff. Zalem was scared to look down, but when he did he saw Blake and King George holding onto a tree root. Zalem quickly grabbed the rope that he had in his bag. He tied it tightly to a sturdy tree. He then wrapped the rope around his waist, and he began to lower himself down the cliff to them.

They watched him lower himself, and then he reached them and tied the rope around Blake's waist. Zalem tried to grab King George so he could try to get him to go in front of him. They then realized that the rope may not be able to hold three people, especially since King George was a heavy-set man. So Blake and Zalem climbed up, and

Zalem lowered the rope. Then Zalem and Blake pulled the King up.

"Pull faster. Hurry, we have to get him up here," said Blake as he tugged harder.

"No, not too fast or the rope may break," said Zalem, as they both continued to pull. Finally, King George was up the cliff. Blake hugged his father. He was so happy that they were both OK.

"I love you. You're the only son I have left," said King George.

"I love you too, father. I am so sorry for everything," said Blake. They walked forward together as Zalem heard a sound. He saw a guy shoot an arrow in their direction. Zalem yelled and told them to duck. They all ducked but the King wasn't quick enough. He was hit directly in the heart.

Zalem turned back to try to see where the man was who shot the arrow, but he had vanished. Zalem turned back around and realized that the King had been hit. "Father, No. Zalem, help me! We have to move him," said Blake as he tried to pick his father up.

"We can't," said Zalem. He looked at the King

and realized that he would not live.

"He is right, Blake. I am going to die," said King George.

"No, you won't if we can get you back, but Zalem won't help me," said Blake as he began to cry.

"Don't touch me, Zalem. Blake, it's time you learn of a world without me," said King George. Zalem began to shed a few tears.

"Blake, be a great king and tell your mother I love her," said King George as he took his last breaths.

Blake lay over his father's body as he sobbed. Then he looked at Zalem. "How dare you cry when you wouldn't help me?" said Blake angrily.

"I know you are hurting, but he was going to die," said Zalem.

"You don't know that. You didn't even try," said Blake.

"I am not about to argue with you. I refuse to leave his body here. We have to bring his body back to the castle," said Zalem as he went to pick up King George's body.

"Don't touch him," said Blake as he pushed

Zalem away.

"What's your problem? Would you rather leave him here?" asked Zalem.

Blake hated the idea of having Zalem even come near his father or him, but he needed help to carry him back. Blake allowed Zalem to carry his father. They brought him back to where all the men were. The men were all in shock to see that King George was dead. Blake and Zalem explained to them what had happened, even though Blake continuously blamed Zalem. The men gathered up the remainder of their supplies. They then decided to create something to carry the King with. They took one blanket and attached two sticks at the sides that two men could hold and carry the king. Zalem and Sir Luther helped Zion by putting his arms over each one of their shoulders while he hopped on one leg. Sir Adam walked in the front. Next came, Zion with Sir Luther's and Zalem's help. Then behind came Prince Blake with Sir Francis carrying King George. Sir Timothy walked behind to watch for danger.

They walked and finally saw the castle. When they arrived at the castle, King Joseph and everyone were informed. King George's wife traveled earlier in the day and arrived that night, so they could return home all together in the morning. Everyone left their chambers to meet them in the main hall. Lillianna quickly went with Zion to seek medical attention in the castle. King George's wife, Queen Arianna, was overwhelmed with tears, and she screamed when she saw her husband lying there, dead.

Blake tried to explain that it was Zalem's fault, but she wouldn't hear it. She blamed Blake for everything after she heard the story. "How dare you try to blame everyone else but yourself? This is the same thing you did when your brother, Augustus died, Blake. I do not wish to hear anything else from you. I am alone now. Are you happy?" said Queen Arianna. She began to walk away, then turned back around and looked at Blake. "Now you have to live with two deaths on your hands. I hope you can live with yourself."

Zalem didn't wish to speak to anyone, so he just went into his chambers. King Joseph followed his son, and heard the sound of Zalem destroying his chambers. King Joseph grabbed him, and Zalem began to cry on his shoulder. "It's all my fault," said Zalem. "It's no one's fault. Nobody knew those thieves were coming," said King Joseph. "King George was wrong. I cannot be King. I can't even keep everyone alive or not injured," said Zalem as he sat on his bed. "Stop, Zalem. This is horrible, but don't take King George's death for granted," said the King.

"What do you mean?" asked Zalem as the King sat down next to him.

"I mean that you should learn from his death," said his father.

"How?" asked Zalem.

"You only have one life to live, Zalem. Make the best of it," said the King.

"You're correct," said Zalem, wiping away all his tears.

The King got up and picked up Zalem's crown that Zalem had knocked down. He then dusted it off and put it on the dresser. "This crown is temporary. The one on my head will be yours soon. I want you to be the one to have it, Zalem. I wouldn't choose anyone else, but you have to choose yourself as well, Zalem," said his father. He gave him a hug while Zalem still sat on the bed. Then the King walked toward the door and said, "I will send someone to clean up this mess. Cheer up. Goodnight, son"

Zalem looked at his father and said, "Goodnight." Zalem began to think of a way to move on from all of this. He got an idea when Rebecca came into the chambers to clean it.

"Hello, Prince Zalem," said Rebecca as she bowed.

"Hello, Rebecca...Rebecca, I have a question," said Zalem.

"Yes, Prince Zalem," answered Rebecca as she came to him.

"I want your honest opinion about Lady Cassandra," asked Zalem.

"I don't mean to be rude, Prince Zalem, but I don't know if my opinion matters," said

Rebecca.

"It really does matter," said Zalem.

"Well, she seems like she truly is selfish and doesn't care about your kingdom," said Rebecca.

"Thank you for your honesty, Rebecca. I am going to bathe and think," said Zalem.

"Yes, Prince Zalem. Do you want me to draw your bath?" asked Rebecca.

"No, I can do it myself, but thanks for asking," said Zalem.

As Zalem bathed, he thought a lot and came up with an idea. He grabbed a towel and ran out of the bath chamber to talk to Rebecca. He saw Rebecca about to walk out of his bed chambers. "Rebecca...Rebecca, please wait," said Zalem.

"Yes, Prince Zalem," answered Rebecca. She smiled from embarrassment when she saw him in his towel.

"I hope this isn't uncomfortable, seeing me without a shirt, but can you please prepare my stuff so I can go to visit Cassandra's family? I am taking what you said into consideration. Please tell her that we will be

going first thing in the morning," said Zalem.
"Yes, Prince Zalem," answered Rebecca as
she blushed and walked away. She almost
walked into the wall, and then she almost
tripped. "I'm OK," she said.

Zalem walked into his closet, where he
began to quietly laugh.

Chapter 9

The next day, Zalem awoke ready to go and meet Cassandra's family. Cassandra wasn't as happy as Zalem. She was upset because she didn't really want to do this, and she was surprised that he *did* really want to do it.

They met outside. "Good morning," said Zalem to Cassandra as the guards loaded up the carriage.

"Hello," answered Cassandra sharply. Zalem grabbed her hand to help her into the carriage. Then Zalem climbed in, and they sat silently as Cassandra fanned herself. Zalem was really excited to get a chance to see the people from the kingdom and how they lived. The carriage passed a lot of farmland and pine trees. Zalem enjoyed the aroma of all the flowers, as they made their way into the town. As the carriage was moving, Zalem saw two kids playing. Their ball went into a mean old man's house. He refused to give it back to them. Zalem got upset. "Stop the carriage, please," he said. The guards stopped the carriage.

"Why are we stopping?" Cassandra asked.

"You don't have to come out if you don't want to," said Zalem as he walked out of the carriage.

Cassandra answered quietly, "Wouldn't dream of it." She fanned herself and remained in the carriage. Cassandra decided to watch.

Zalem waved to the children and walked past them to the old man. Everyone began to bow when they saw Zalem. "You weren't going to keep that ball for yourself, were you?" asked Zalem.

"No, Prince Zalem, never," the old man answered, bowing and handing Zalem the ball.

Zalem turned around and told everyone to stop bowing and return to the way they were. He then walked to the children and kneeled down to their height. "Here's your ball," said Zalem as he handed it to them. The little girl hugged Zalem, and the boy hugged him at the same time. Then the little girl gave him a kiss on his cheek. In that kiss, Zalem was really happy and began to feel better. At that moment, Zalem realized that being king would come with a lot of ups and downs, but maybe it would be worth it. Zalem decided to take some time and play with the children. They kicked the ball back and forth to one another. After five minutes, Zalem had to leave. Before he left, he went to the old man and said, "Please don't take their ball from them, or anything else, again."

The old man said, "Yes, my Prince," as he bowed.

Zalem then turned away and left. He got into the carriage, but not before Cassandra gave her sly remark. "Well, it took you long enough," she said. Zalem ignored her, and they continued on to the factory.

Zalem, Cassandra, and two of the guards walked into the factory. Outside it was very muddy, and inside, the factory smelled strange. Cassandra hated every minute of this, but continued, not knowing what to expect. When Cassandra walked in she saw her father in a really nice office. "Hello Father, I would like you to meet Prince Zalem," said Cassandra.

"Good morning. It is an honor to meet you," said Mr. Cruze. He got up out of his chair and bowed. He rose back up and spoke again. "I am sorry you came all this way to meet my family because Cassandra's mother and brothers aren't here," he said.

"Well, we aren't here for that. We are here to see the factory," answered Cassandra.

"What Cassandra means to say is that it is sad they aren't here. I wanted to meet them and see the factory as well," said Zalem.

"Really?" replied Mr. Cruze in a surprised tone.

"I know," answered Cassandra as she

winked, then smiled in agreement.

"I hope you aren't upset that I came. Would you be willing to give me a tour?" said Zalem.

"Yes, Prince Zalem," said Mr. Cruze. He bowed again and began the tour. As they walked out of the office, Zalem saw many underdressed workers. Zalem couldn't believe they walked out of that nice office into a shabby place. They had reached the first room of the tour.

"This is where the clothing is made," said Mr. Cruze. Zalem saw that the workers were mostly on sewing machines. For the most part, it was a very quiet room. Then they all continued on from there outside, where he saw men and women picking cotton. "After we look at this, there is much more to see," said Mr. Cruze. Cassandra hated that she had to walk through the mud, but she was trying to keep quiet and not let Zalem know how she truly felt.

Mr. Cruze began to show Zalem the cotton before it is picked. When one of the men that was working passed by all of them, he accidentally tripped in front of Cassandra and got mud on her dress. Cassandra got so mad that she slapped the man in the face and he hit the ground hard. "You idiot," screamed Cassandra. She began to raise her leg to kick him.

At that moment a rage went through Zalem's body as he yelled, "If you kick that man, I promise to chop your leg off with my sword." He gripped the handle of his sword.

"You dare threaten me?" replied Cassandra, in shock.

"She doesn't mean that," said Mr. Cruze.

"Yes, I do. That man is a fool. He shouldn't work here if he is unable to keep his balance. He deserves to be beaten," said Cassandra.

Zalem dropped the cotton and pulled his sword. Zalem didn't expect this from Cassandra. Mr. Cruze blocked his daughter as Zalem approached her. "Either remove yourself, or the guards will move you," said Zalem in a very angry and aggressive voice to Mr. Cruze. Mr. Cruze wouldn't hear it, so Zalem said calmly, "OK then, guards." The guards pulled Mr. Cruze away, and then Zalem approached Cassandra. He put his sword at her neck. "You dare so much as raise any part of your body to hurt someone, and I will personally make sure that it is dismantled. Do I make myself clear?" said Zalem softly, but aggressively. Cassandra didn't answer, so Zalem pushed the sword a little further and asked again, "Do you understand me?"

Cassandra answered, "Yes, I do."

Zalem replied, "Good." He told the guards to let down Mr. Cruze, and help the man up off the ground. He removed the sword from Cassandra's neck and it left a mark. Zalem turned to the worker who had fallen when he began to speak.

"Thank you, my Prince, I really do appreciate what you have done. No one has ever stood up for me before."

Zalem then asked, "What is your name?" Zalem stared at a scar on the man's left cheek, across his cheekbone.

"My name is Henry Chaslin," said the man. Henry had much darker skin than Zalem.

"OK, Henry, nice to meet you," said Zalem as he stretched out his hand to shake Henry's hand.

"The pleasure is all mine," said Henry.

"Please stay here and listen to this; I have an idea," said Prince Zalem.

"Yes, my Prince," answered Henry.

Zalem turned to the guards and Cassandra and Mr. Cruze and said, "I want the Cruze family name removed from this business."

Mr. Cruze leaped forward and said, "You can't do that," but the guards pulled him back.

"Yes, I can. Since I walked in, I realized something was wrong here. You treat these people like trash," said Zalem.

Mr. Cruze calmed down and decided to speak to Zalem. "Not to upset you, Sire, but no, we do not. Cassandra has never seen the factory before. This is all I have."

Zalem responded, "I understand that..." He began to think, and then said, "Everyone stay here." He walked inside to talk to some of the workers in the sewing room. When he walked in, he changed his mind and decided to ask everyone in the room instead of one or two people.

"Everyone please, can I have your attention? Can you stop what you're doing and give me your full attention?" asked Zalem as they all dropped everything and turned to him. "I need you to answer honestly as I ask you these questions, OK?" asked Zalem. Some nodded their heads "yes," and others answered verbally. "Thank you. So, please raise your hand if any member of the Cruze family has ever treated you badly," said Zalem.

All of the fifty or so people in the room raised their hands. Zalem shook his head in frustration, and then asked another question. "OK, everyone put down your hands. Answer one more question. Raise your hand if they ever hit you with anything?"

Everyone raised their hands, except three people. "OK, thank you for your honestly. This is what's going to happen. The Cruze family is going to step down as owners of this business," said Zalem as he walked outside. Outside the door, Zalem heard the excitement of the people from the room and smiled.

Zalem then returned to where he left the two guards, Henry, Mr. Cruze, and Cassandra. He walked up to Mr. Cruze and said, "Exactly what I said before is going to happen. Have your things out of here by tonight. To help your family, I promise this: You will always be able to become a worker here for the rest of your life. That goes for your entire family, but none of you can own it ever again," said Zalem. Then he turned to Henry. "Henry."

"Yes, Sire," answered Henry.

"I have a job for you. I want you to get better pay, and work with the person I am going to put in charge of this business. For now, though, I need you to run it until I get that person. What do you say?" asked Zalem as Cassandra stormed off in anger.

Henry was at a loss for words, but quickly gathered his thoughts and said, "Yes, sire, thank you. I would hug you, but I don't want to get mud on you."

"Give me a handshake, and we'll hug another day," said Zalem as they shook hands. Zalem then turned around and gathered his guards and began to walk away. Then he remembered one more thing and turned around. "Oh yeah, Mr. Cruze, the same thing I told your daughter goes for you and your entire family. You should warn them so they don't lose any limbs," said Zalem as he walked away.

Mr. Cruze began to cry and fell down on his knees in the mud. Zalem then yelled back to him, "Thanks for the tour." Zalem returned to the carriage and left that place, hoping that one day when he returned, it would be an amazing visit.

Zalem returned home feeling like a weight had been lifted off of his shoulders. He now had only two women to choose from. Zalem began to wonder how he did not see through Cassandra. He decided to go and check on Evangeline and Veronica. While Zalem was walking down the hall, he ran into Rebecca close to the library. Zalem approached from behind her and said, "Good evening, Rebecca."

Rebecca, startled, replied, "Oh, good evening, Prince Zalem," as she calmed down."

"I took your advice, Rebecca," said Zalem.

"What advice, Prince Zalem?" said Rebecca, very puzzled.

"With Cassandra; I got rid of her," said Zalem.

"Oh no, Prince Zalem, I didn't mean to get in between you and Cassandra's relationship," said Rebecca, very sadly.

"No, I paid more attention to her, and she showed her true colors. Trust me, she's not the woman for me," said Zalem.

Rebecca began to smile and said, "Then that's good, I am glad. You seem happy."

Zalem replied, "I really am, Rebecca. When King George died I was so upset, but now I realize that I have no time to waste. I have a bride to choose," as he stood firmly.

"If you don't mind me asking, do you feel confident about these two women?" asked Rebecca.

"I don't really know yet. I'll decide today when I spend time with them. I wanted to ask you something," said Zalem.

"You can ask me anything, Prince Zalem," said Rebecca as she bowed again.

"How do you feel when you are around Evangeline and Veronica? Before you answer, please, just tell me honestly about them," asked Zalem.

"Well, Veronica is a very sweet girl; she treats everyone so wonderfully," said Rebecca. She paused.

"What's wrong?" asked Zalem.

"I just don't like talking badly about people," said Rebecca.

"Please, Rebecca, tell me what you think," said Zalem as he grabbed her hands with both of his.

Rebecca let go of his hands and answered. "OK. Evangeline is really rude to all the workers. She acts very different in front of you."

Zalem was in shock, and at that moment he heard someone coming down the hall. Zalem quickly realized that it was Evangeline; he then turned to Rebecca and said, "Don't let her know I am here." He ran into the closest room to him, which was the library, and listened.

"Good evening, Lady Evangeline," said Rebecca.

Evangeline turned and looked at Rebecca with disgust and said, "You workers make me sick. The royal family treats all of you so well. When I become queen, that will change." Zalem then walked out of the library and slammed the door out of anger. Evangeline turned and saw Zalem. At that moment her attitude changed to become more cheerful. "Prince Zalem. When did you return?" asked Evangeline.

"I returned early, after I decided to leave Cassandra with her family. I made them leave the business. I want nothing to do with any of them," said Zalem in a disappointed tone.

"Oh, I'm sorry you're sad that you let her go. But there was another side of her that you didn't see. She was very rude," said Evangeline.

Rebecca began to walk away; she felt like she didn't belong there. "Rebecca, don't leave. I want you to hear this. Evangeline, you need to apologize to Rebecca," said Zalem very firmly.

"You're joking, right? She's the help...a worker, nothing more than that," replied Evangeline, laughing.

"Rebecca is a good person who deserves to be treated better than that. You know what, Evangeline? Never mind. Just please leave the castle," said Zalem calmly, as he began to walk away from Evangeline.

"Are you leaving me?" asked Evangeline.

"You're definitely not the woman for me. You are very selfish, and you mistreat others. I am looking for a better person to be the queen. I would be crazy to even believe that you could be worthy of that," said Zalem.

"Zalem, wait," said Evangeline, as she grabbed his hand.

He removed her hand with his other hand and said, "I'd rather you just leave. It would be embarrassing to watch you get thrown out of the palace, and it wouldn't be that pretty to watch," said Zalem.

Evangeline angrily walked away and went to

her chambers to pack. Rebecca then turned to Zalem and said, "I hope I didn't ruin your chances with her."

He replied, "You did nothing wrong. Evangeline was just not the woman for me. She showed me who she really was. You helped me to do that so I could look past her pretty face." He looked upset.

"Prince Zalem, you're a really good guy, and you will become a great king. I could never handle that job," said Rebecca.

"Thank you, Rebecca, it means a lot to hear you say that. I was starting to think I was horrible to her," said Zalem.

"She's going to be fine, Prince Zalem," answered Rebecca as they both smiled.

"Well, I'm going to check on Zion, then maybe go and see Veronica. Thank you for listening," said Zalem.

"You're welcome; it's my pleasure," said Rebecca.

"No, the pleasure is mine," said Zalem, as he bowed and kissed her hand. Zalem went to Zion's chambers but couldn't find him. He saw Isabelle cleaning up and asked, "Have you seen Zion?"

She replied, "Yes, I saw him last with Lillianna. They were headed to the lake."

Zalem replied, "Thanks," and went to the lake to meet them. Isabelle loved to see Zalem happy, which wasn't quite often. When Zalem got to the lake, he saw Lillianna sitting down with Zion's head on her lap. She was playing with his hair. Zion's leg was wrapped in gauze.

"Hey, Zalem," said Lillianna as he leaned down to let her give him a kiss on the cheek. Zalem then sat down with them. "Hey, how are you?" Zalem asked Zion as they shook hands.

"I am great, except for my leg, but I am as strong as an ox. So what brings you out here?" asked Zion.

"I came to check on you and see what the doctor said," replied Zalem.

"Well, I won't be able to walk for about two or three months," answered Zion.

"Yeah, Zion and I were just talking about that," said Lillianna.

"I am so sorry that all of this even

happened," said Zalem.

"No, it's OK. We had no idea that all of this was going to happen. At least I am still alive. All I am sorry about is that I won't be able to help Lillianna with the pregnancy," said Zion.

"Yeah, I know. Zion has been beating himself up over that," said Lillianna.

"OK, then it's my job to help you, Lillianna until you get on your feet, Zion." said Zalem.

"As great as that would be, you have too much on your plate," said Lillianna, rubbing her belly.

"Yeah, between finding a bride and becoming king, it's a lot on your plate," said Zion.

"I guess you're right, but I will promise to do as much as I can for you before the baby is born—and after as well," said Zalem.

"Anyway, how has it been going with the dating?" said Lillianna.

"Not easy, but I am down to one girl...Veronica," said Zalem.

"What? Well, what happened to Cassandra and Evangeline?" asked Lillianna.

Zalem explained how he had dismissed

Cassandra and Evangeline, and Lillianna replied, "I am glad that you saw through both of them. You need to find love and a great queen." She leaned back.

"Yes, I'm glad as well, but I am tired of dating. I hope Veronica is the one," said Zalem.

"Relax, you'll make the right decision," said Zion.

"Yes, Zion is right. It may look hard now, but you'll get through it. I am always going to be behind you with whoever you choose, as long as you're in love," said Lillianna.

She hugged Zalem as she felt the baby kick. "Oh, Zion, Zalem, put your hands here. Feel the baby kick," said Lillianna as she grabbed both of their hands and placed them on her stomach. "Isn't that amazing?" said Lillianna.

"Yes, it is," said Zalem. He watched Lillianna and Zion together and realized that he wanted the same life: to sit by the lake with his wife and feel their baby kick. Zalem wanted to be happy. "Well, I am going to go inside and check on Veronica," said Zalem.

"OK, see you later at dinner," said Lillianna. Zalem walked away and felt like he was at peace when he saw his family. Zalem walked inside and found Veronica sitting by the windowsill by the front of the castle, which looked out at the garden. He walked up to her and said "Hey, how are you? May I sit here?"

"Yes, sure, sit," said Veronica as Zalem sat down. "How are you doing, after getting your heart broken twice?" said Veronica.

"I am great, and I did not get my heart broken," said Zalem.

"You sure? You really liked Evangeline," said Veronica.

"How do you know that?" asked Zalem.

"Your lips and her lips never got tired of one another," said Veronica. Zalem laughed.

"That does not mean I have love in my heart for her. When you love a woman you want to be with her for the rest of her life. So I will not say I love a woman until then," said Zalem.

"Wow, until the end of *her* life, not *yours*...OK, then, let me ask you: how do you feel about us?" asked Veronica.

"What do you mean?" asked Zalem.

"I want to know how you feel about you and I together," asked Veronica.

"I don't really know how to answer that, because I don't really know if I am in a place to judge my own feelings. I have been making a lot of mistakes about my feelings with Cassandra and Evangeline," said Zalem.

Inside of Veronica's head, she definitely agreed with him. "I think you're a great judge of character; that's why you left Cassandra and Evangeline. You'll do just fine. I am tired, though, and I think I am going to retire," said Veronica.

"Wait, before you do that, can I ask you something? Tomorrow I want us to spend more time together. I am really interested in getting to know you better," asked Zalem.

"That sounds great," answered Veronica as she gave him a kiss on the cheek and went off to bed. Zalem stayed there and sat down. He continued to look out the window.

Isabelle walked in and wasn't expecting to

see Zalem sitting there.

"Sorry, I didn't know anyone would be here. I'll be leaving," said Isabelle as she turned to walk away.

"No, you don't have to leave. You're welcome to stay. Why don't you join me and sit for a while?" said Zalem. Isabelle agreed and sat down on the cushion.

She opened her book to read, and she realized that Zalem was really pondering something. She decided to ask, "So what's on your mind?"

He replied, "Why does everyone want to know what's on my mind? I don't even know how they know I have something on my mind."

"Well, if I sat in silence and gazed out the window, I would only hope someone would ask me," said Isabelle. Zalem began to laugh, and she smiled.

Zalem smiled and replied, "Yeah, I guess you're right. I have just been thinking of Veronica."

"Really?" said Isabelle.

"Yeah, I wonder if she's really the one for me.

I don't want women like Cassandra and Evangeline, and I can't decide if she is like them or not," said Zalem.

"You're really overthinking all of this. You will get the wife you deserve. Zalem, just be patient. Everyone knows you are amazing," said Isabelle.

"Thanks, Isabelle, it honestly feels so good when I am around you. You are one of the few people that aren't expecting anything from me," said Zalem. He smiled and asked Isabelle a question. "Remember when we talked before about your family? Tell me about them, please." He watched Isabelle gaze into the moonlight. Their eyes met, and he took her hand and caressed her face, then pulled her in for a kiss. They got deep into the kiss, so deep that Isabelle began to develop a deep emotional attachment to Zalem.

Then Isabelle dropped the book that was sitting on her lap, and they both snapped back to reality. "I am so sorry...we shouldn't have done that," said Isabelle.

"No, it was me...I am sorry. My head isn't on

right. I can't just go kissing people," said
Zalem as Isabelle picked up her book,
stuttered her words and awkwardly ran off,
holding her lips. Zalem sat in silence,
puzzled by his actions but happy with the
kiss. He couldn't forget about it all night
long.

Chapter 10

The following day Zalem arose to a peaceful morning, after a beautiful kiss the night before. He was filled with joy. Then there was a knock at the door and Prince Zalem answered, "Come in."

It was Sir Luther; he bowed and then spoke. "Good Morning Prince Zalem, sorry to bother you but Princess Veronica awaits you in the main hall."

Zalem quickly snapped back to reality and realized his fantasies were over. "OK, tell her that I am getting ready. Thank you, Sir Luther," he said. Zalem rushed to get himself together, then walked out to the main hall to meet Veronica. "Good morning, my lady," said Zalem as he bowed and kissed her hand.

"Good morning," replied Veronica as she curtsied.

"Let's go to the courtyard for tea," said Zalem.

"We can't; it is raining," said Veronica.

"Fine, then let's go out to the foyer. It will be just as private," said Zalem. They held hands and walked together, looking at all the portraits once again. They reached the foyer, where they sat and drank tea at the table. Veronica decided to begin the conversation.

"You never answered my question," she said, sipping her tea.

"What question?" asked Zalem.

"How do you feel about us?" asked Veronica.

"You are right, I never did answer you," said Zalem as he sipped his tea.

"Well, tell me," insisted Veronica.

"I am beginning to feel really great about us. Now I want to just see where it goes," said Zalem.

"I am glad to hear that." said Veronica. She pulled him in for a kiss.

At that moment Isabelle walked into the room to look for her bracelet. Isabelle had a smile on her face, but then she saw them kissing. Before Isabelle could be seen, she quietly ran out of the foyer. She got out into the hall and by accident dropped a glass bottle on the ground. Lillianna was passing through the hall and saw the bottle slip right out of her hand. Then Isabelle dropped onto her knees and began to cry.

"What's wrong, Isabelle?" asked Lillianna as she ran up to her to help pick up the glass.

"I am sorry I broke the bottle. I'll clean it up right away," she said as she got up quickly to get a broom and dust pan.

"Stop, Isabelle, and come here, please," said Lillianna as Lillianna got up. Isabelle turned around and walked to her. "I will get someone to clean it up." said Lillianna as Rebecca walked by. "Rebecca, can you please clean this up for Isabelle? I am going to have a talk with her." Lillianna grabbed Isabelle's hand.

"Thank you, Rebecca," said Isabelle, attempting to wipe away her tears.

"You're welcome," answered Rebecca as she attended to the glass, realizing Isabelle's traumatic state.

Lillianna and Isabelle walked and found two chairs in the hall. Lillianna handed Isabelle her handkerchief and she wiped away all her tears. "Now, please explain to me why you're crying," said Lillianna.

"You are going to think I am stupid," said Isabelle.

"No, I won't; just please tell me. I am very worried about you. I rarely see you cry, so please tell me," said Lillianna.

"Last night I went downstairs to the windowsill by the garden to read, and Zalem was there. I was going to leave, but Zalem told me I should stay. We began to talk and one thing lead to another, and we kissed," explained Isabelle.

"Well, that's a good thing. Isn't it?" asked Lillianna.

"Yeah, at least I thought it was," said Isabelle.

"What do you mean?" asked Lillianna.

"I just saw him kissing Veronica. I am so

confused. I don't know why he kissed me," said Isabelle.

"I get it now; I am so sorry," said Lillianna. "Please don't let him know I told you, OK?" asked Isabelle.

"OK, I promise I won't," said Lillianna. Inside of Lillianna's head, she was confused as well. "Isabelle, cancel what you have to do today. We're going to have a girl's day. Just you and I," she said.

"OK, then," said Isabelle.

"Please stop crying; you look horrible," said Lillianna.

As they both laughed, Isabelle replied, "I know you didn't tell me I look ugly when I cry. When you broke your Mother's favorite vase, who was ugly then?" Isabelle impersonated what Lillianna looked like when she cried, and then they both got up laughing, talking as they walked away.

Meanwhile, Veronica and Zalem continued their very happy day. Zalem was beginning to get to know Veronica and really develop feelings for her. "So tell me, Veronica. When you were growing up in the royal life, did you always want to become queen?" he asked.

"I wasn't too excited about becoming queen, but when I watched my parents and how they ruled the kingdom, it helped me to realize what I wanted," said Veronica.

"Good answer," said Zalem as Veronica smiled. "So, how was your childhood growing up?" Zalem asked.

"It wasn't great, because my parents fought a lot. My mom was very pushy and my dad did not want to hear her sometimes. Their arguing made a happy kingdom, but a sad child," said Veronica.

"I don't understand how that works. You make them sound awful," said Zalem, very puzzled.

"By them acting that way, it motivated me to become better than them. The truth is that when my mom passed away, life became much easier for my Dad and me," said Veronica, even though her Mother was still alive.

"There seems to be a lot behind your childhood," said Zalem.

"Yeah, there is, but it helped me to figure everything out. I want to rule, to help my people, and have an amazing husband and king. I want my husband and I to listen to one another and love one another," said Veronica.

"That's the same thing I am looking for," said Zalem with delight.

"That's good to know. Maybe we can make this work after all," said Veronica.

"Yeah, just maybe," said Zalem. They were about to kiss, but Zalem remembered something he wanted to ask her. "Oh yeah, I wanted to ask you about your father, and I would really love to meet him. Do you think that is possible?" he asked.

As Veronica started to answer, she was interrupted by Sir Nicholas coming into the room. He bowed and said, "Sorry for interrupting, Prince Zalem and Princess Veronica, but I was hoping you were ready for training."

Zalem replied, "Yes, of course," as he got up.

"We won't be going outside because of the rain, so we'll do some more bookwork today," said Sir Nicholas.

"OK then, Sir Nicholas," said Zalem. Then he turned to Princess Veronica and said, "Princess Veronica, I will see you later," He kissed her hand and left with Sir Nicholas. Veronica sat and decided to close her eyes and imagine her life. She then heard footsteps and opened her eyes. There was Ethan Blackmore.

"I didn't know anyone was here. Sorry to wake you," said Ethan as he began to leave.

"Please don't leave. Can we just sit and talk?" asked Veronica as she stood up. Ethan turned back and sat down with Veronica. "But you're a princess. It feels so wrong to be sitting here," he said.

"Don't feel that way. I want the people around me to look at me like I am a regular person," said Veronica.

"Okay, then I will," Ethan said. "How have you been?"

"Really great...I have really missed you," said Veronica.

"Missed me?" asked Ethan.

"Yes," answered Veronica.

"Why would you miss me? You barley know me," replied Ethan in a wondering tone.

"I know I barley know you, but since I first saw you, I can't get the image of your face out of my head," said Veronica. Veronica then remembered her mother and what she told her and decided to leave before she made things worse. "Well, I am going," said Veronica. But she was interrupted with a kiss from Ethan.

At that moment, Zalem walked by. He was shocked and confused to see Ethan and Veronica kissing. Zalem made up a lie to Sir Nicholas, so he could go and see Veronica quickly. Zalem slowly walked away in silence. He didn't know what to say or do, so he just went back to his training. After he was gone and unseen, Veronica got very intense with the kiss and then all of a sudden she hopped back, in shock. "Oh my, what are we doing?" said Veronica as she jumped out of her seat.

"I don't know what happened," said Ethan.

"What do you mean you don't know—you kissed me," answered Veronica as Ethan stood up.

"Yeah, I guess I did, but I don't understand what happened," he said.

"I know you're not uneducated, so clearly you can comprehend a kiss," said Veronica.

"Yes, I kissed you, but you liked it," answered Ethan.

"This is not about me, it's about you," said Veronica.

"I disagree with that. I may have kissed you, but you kissed me back," said Ethan as he looked at her awkwardly. "Am I right?" he continued.

"Don't look at me like that. We did both kiss," answered Veronica as she sat back down.

"So what does that kiss mean?" asked Ethan as he sat back down.

"I don't know," said Veronica. She stared into space as she thought about the kiss and touched her lips.

Ethan was confused and was beginning to wonder if it was a mistake. "Would you want to do it again?" he asked as he touched underneath her chin and lead it back to his face. Veronica was lost in his eyes. When she thought about her mother again and snapped back to reality.

"We can't be together. The kiss was a mistake. I love Zalem and we have something very special together," answered Veronica as she got up and began to walk out the room.

"How can you say that? You barley know him," asked Ethan.

She turned around and answered, "I don't know you, either. It's none of your business anyway. Just stay away from me; it will never work." Veronica walked out the room and then turned around and stood in the doorway.

Ethan stood up and looked toward her leaving and said, "You invited me into the foyer, but I apologize for my actions."

"I am so sorry for mine as well. Good-bye," answered Veronica. She began to head down the hall to her chambers. But she turned around and ran back to Ethan and kissed him again. "This is good-bye," said Veronica as she left. She got to her chambers, and she closed her door and then locked it. After that, she sat down behind the door and began to cry. Veronica was so upset and didn't know what to do.

Then she heard her mother's voice again. "What's wrong? Why are you crying?" asked her mother as she put her hand on Veronica's shoulder.

"I don't want to talk to you about it. Just please go away," said Veronica. She got up from behind the door and wiped away her tears. She walked away from her as her mother followed Veronica and began to play with her hair. "What's wrong? You know I love you, and..."

At that moment, Veronica slapped her mother's hand away and said, "If you love me, then don't make me marry Prince Zalem. I don't love him." Veronica then walked away and sat on her bed.

"You know you can't do that. You have to marry Zalem," answered her mother as she shook her head.

"Why do you hang around me if you want to continue to make my life miserable?" said

Veronica. Her mother sat down next to her. She raised Veronica's chin up to look at her face, and Veronica thought of Ethan. Then her mother looked into her eyes and said, "You're in love."

"No, I am not," said Veronica as she turned her face and got up. Her mother followed her and grabbed her hand.

Veronica turned around, and her mother said, "Not with Zalem. So who are you in love with?"

"I told you that there is nobody else," said Veronica.

"Veronica, don't you dare lie to me. If you don't tell me now and I find out later, then I will make sure he disappears," said her mother as she pushed Veronica against the wall. She pressed her body against Veronica's and held her there.

Veronica was so scared, she said, "Promise me you won't do anything to hurt him in any way."

Veronica's mother replied in a demanding voice, "Fine, I won't hurt him. Now tell me."

"It is Ethan Blackmore, Prince Zion's

brother," answered Veronica.

Veronica's mother pushed her against the wall harder and said, "I advise you to get him out of your head. He has nothing to offer you. He is not a prince, or even wealthy."

Veronica replied, "Is being wealthy all you think about, mother? What about love?"

Her mother let her down off the wall and replied, "Look at me as an example. I followed my heart and married your father; now look at where it got me. It was a waste of time, but I am now rich and so are you. You have me to thank for the good life you have."

"He wasted his life with you. You weren't even worth his heart. You were just a peasant and he made you something. And look at how you repay him. You're forgetting that I don't care for this life," Veronica screamed.

Her mother began to point her finger and yell. Veronica was walking backward as her mother walked toward her, angrily saying, "You're such a spoiled girl, Veronica. I made sure you got everything you wanted. You owe me this. All I ask you to do is to marry Zalem. Is it that hard to do?"

"You should have stayed dead to us. Our lives were so much better when you were dead," said Veronica. Her mother slapped her in the face.

Veronica's face was in pain but she didn't care, she took the slap with pride and then continued to listen as he Mother spoke.

"Don't you dare talk to me like that. Remember, I am your mother," as she walked away from Veronica.

"He wants to meet my family. How will I show him that?" said Veronica.

"Don't worry about that, I will figure it out. Just do as I say and listen," answered her mother. Then she told Veronica the plan.

While Veronica was in her chambers, Ethan picked himself up and went to meet King Joseph because he had been summoned by him. He walked into the throne room and bowed and said, "Good evening, King Joseph; Queen Tianna." He stood back at attention.

"Good evening, Ethan," said the King.

"Good evening," said the Queen, while she was sewing a baby hat.

"I called you here today because of Zalem. Do you remember the Cruze family, Ethan?" asked the King.

"Yes I do, sire," answered Ethan. He began to worry that Zalem knew about him kissing Veronica and wanted to kill him. Then he began to relax when he heard about the Cruze family.

"Well, Zalem went over to their factory and got into a little confrontation. Anyway, to make the story short, he dismissed them as owners, and we both thought you would be best suited to own it now," said the King.

"Me? Me?" said Ethan, who was very shocked, but happy.

"It could be a family investment. This way, your family will never be out of money. It was Zalem's idea, but I back it one hundred percent," said the King.

"Wow, I am honored, and thank you so much. I accept," said Ethan. He felt bad for kissing Zalem's girl.

"That's great. When you get there, you'll find

a man named Henry Chaslin that Zalem left in charge. That man and you will work side-by-side, and he will teach you the business. But you're the boss," said the King.

Ethan thanked him and gave him a handshake. The King pulled him in and gave him a hug. Ethan was off to begin a new life.

Later that night after Zalem was done training, he decided to go for a walk. Zalem was trying to clear his head to figure out what he wanted. He didn't understand why he had kissed Isabelle and still kept Veronica around. He wondered how it would look to be with a woman who wasn't royalty, and even worse, a servant. As Zalem thought, he walked outside around the castle grounds. After that, he decided to walk inside. He then saw the library doors and walked in. Zalem heard a noise and continued walking in. He saw Lillianna looking at the books. Zalem approached her and said, "Hey."

She turned her head and said, "Hey."

Then they both blurted out, "Can I talk to you?" at the same time.

"You first," said Zalem.

"No, you first," said Lillianna.

"OK. I wanted to talk to you about Veronica and Isabelle," said Zalem.

"Why those two?" asked Lillianna.

"I know I am wrong for this, but I kissed Isabelle, and after that, I kissed Veronica. Then I saw Veronica kissing Ethan, so I don't even know what that means," said Zalem, as Lillianna's jaw dropped.

"You kissed...And she kissed...And then...WOW. I don't even know what to say," replied Lillianna.

"That's crazy; you never run out of words. Lillianna, I don't know what to do. Tell me, please," said Zalem.

Lillianna remained speechless, so Zalem tapped her and called her name. She then processed everything and said, "Wow...,"and smiled.

"Please give me more words then that," said Zalem.

"OK, well, first thing is, you need to sit down and be honest with yourself. Who do you love, Zalem?" asked Lillianna, as they both went and sat down.

"I don't know; but one thing I do know, I don't want to make things awkward between Isabelle and me. Isabelle is a great friend, but Veronica seems like she may like, or even truly love, Ethan. But at the same time, she wants me," said Zalem.

"Exactly, so if you want to see where it goes with Isabelle, then do that. But it sounds like Veronica may have already made her choice," answered Lillianna.

"You're right," replied Zalem.

"I know I am. You wouldn't have come and asked me, if I was always wrong," said Lillianna. She got up and grabbed the book she wanted.

"Well, I think that's wrong, because it was your idea to date all three women, remember?" said Zalem, laughing.

Lillianna laughed, too, and agreed, "I could be wrong, sometimes." She began to walk out, then turned back and said, "Zalem, just think and you'll make the correct decision about what makes you happy, while still considering others." She walked out of the library and into her chambers with Royal. Zalem thought about everything and made his final decision to confront Veronica. He would work on his relationship with both girls to see where they would go. Zalem grew tired and looked at the time. He realized that it was late, and he decided to retire for the night. The next day would be hard for him, but he knew what he had to do.

Chapter 11

The following day Zalem decided to get up early and go to Veronica's chambers to talk. Then he ran into Isabelle in the main hall. They awkwardly said hello to one another, as Isabelle wasn't expecting to say much. She was about to walk away, and Zalem said, "I want to talk to you." He looked at her with soft eyes.

"Talk to me about what?" Isabelle asked.

"I want to talk to you about us, and maybe even a relationship, if you're not seeing anyone else right now," said Zalem.

"A relationship?" asked Isabelle, very surprised. Then she paused.

Zalem said, "Yes, with you and me."

Isabelle replied, "I don't know what to say."
Zalem responded happily, "

"I am just a servant. Princes and workers
don't go together," said Isabelle as she
walked further away, rubbing her head.

"I thought about this all night long. I don't
want to be king unless I am happy with you
as my queen. You would be an amazing
queen. You honestly love and care for the
people of this kingdom. I am dumb not to
have noticed this all before," explained
Zalem.

"Don't you want to check with your father,
Lillianna, or maybe even Veronica before you
decide to do this?" asked Isabelle as she
lifted her head up and looked at Zalem.

"No. I am finally going to do something I
want to do; just please give me a chance,"
said Zalem as he grabbed her hand and put
it on his chest.

"What about Veronica? I saw you kissing
her," asked Isabelle as she took her hand
from him and turned away.

He walked toward her and said, "Yes I did,
but how did you know?"

She responded, "I saw the two of you yesterday in the foyer when I went to go and look for my bracelet, but you didn't see me. I can tell you weren't going to tell me, either." Zalem looked surprised that she knew, but she wasn't facing him to see his reaction to what she had just said. He said, "That must have hurt to watch, and I am so sorry. But I know for sure that she doesn't want me, either."

as she walked away. "How do you know that?" said Isabelle.

as he walked closer to her. "I saw her kissing Ethan, and she has feelings for him. I was headed to her chambers now to tell her that we are done," said Zalem as he held her softly from behind.

"Zalem, are you sure about this? It is a very big step, and I am very nervous about it," said Isabelle.

"I am sure. I promise to protect you through it all, no matter what it takes," replied Zalem.

Isabelle turned and looked at him and said, "My heart is saying yes, but my mind is being logical. My father always used to say, 'listen to your heart,' so I am going to try."

Zalem was so happy, that he picked her up in the air and kissed her. "Thank you. Now I am going to talk to Veronica," he said.

"Wait, can we sit and talk for a minute or so? This is all so overwhelming," said Isabelle. They walked out of the main hall and found a seat. "How do you think your family will take the news?" asked Isabelle.

"Everyone, especially Lillianna, will be happy for me, but I don't know what my father will say. All I can do is just hope for the best. What about your family? You always tell me you will explain them, but we never get to it," said Zalem. They both laughed.

"My mother will be excited, and my father will be happier than her, but still nervous," said Isabelle.

"You never mention your father that much. Who is he? What's he like?" asked Zalem. Isabelle began to laugh, and Zalem asked, "Why are you laughing?"

"I am laughing because you've spent so much time with him, you should know him really well," said Isabelle.

"Really, I have? Well, who is your father?" asked Zalem.

"My father is Sir Nicholas, the best father in the world," said Isabelle.

"I can't believe I didn't notice that the two of you are related. I wish I knew before," said Zalem.

"It wouldn't have made a difference if you did know, but anyway, you should be on your way," said Isabelle.

"OK, you're right. I have to get this over with," said Zalem.

"Your saying it like that makes me feel bad for Veronica. I don't want her to get hurt," said Isabelle. They both stood up, and Zalem kissed her on the forehead and grabbed both of her hands with his and looked her in the eyes.

He said, "That's one thing I truly love about you," as they kissed good-bye. Zalem was on his way to see Veronica.

When Zalem reached Veronica's chambers, his entire persona changed from happy to calm and caring, so he could consider her feelings as well. He knocked on the door and Veronica opened it. "Can I come in?" asked Zalem.

"Yes, good morning; excuse me for not being put together," said Veronica as she let him in. She was in her nightgown with no makeup on.

"No, it's OK. I want to talk to you," said Zalem.

"What about?" asked Veronica. "About us...I have been thinking that we should stop thinking that this is going to work, because it won't," said Zalem.

Veronica's smile soon turned to tears. "Why do you want us to end? We are good together," said Veronica.

"I thought we were good together, too, but I fell in love," said Zalem.

"Just not with me...Then with who?" asked Veronica.

"Isabelle," said Zalem.

"Isabelle? The servant over me? But I love you," said Veronica.

"No, you don't, and I chose Isabelle because of you," said Zalem.

"Because of me? How could it be because of me?" asked Veronica, in an aggressive voice.
"I saw you kissing Ethan. I saw how you looked at him, and you love him," said Zalem.
"You saw that? Zalem, I assure you that kiss meant nothing," said Veronica.
"You don't have to lie to me, but if you don't want him, I still know how I feel about Isabelle. I want Isabelle to be the one that will be my wife," said Zalem as he opened the door.
"Zalem, you can't do that," said Veronica as she slammed the door, so he could not leave her chambers.
"And why not?" asked Zalem angrily.
"Because...," said Veronica as she paused and sat down in her chair.
"Why not, Veronica? Why can't I leave you?" asked Zalem, even more aggressive and angry.
"Zalem, do not hate me when I tell you the truth," said Veronica as she began to cry. Zalem crouched down and looked her in the eyes as she continued to sit in the chair.

"Please Veronica; I feel so lost, so just tell me why," said Zalem.

"She kidnapped my father and threatened to kill him if I don't marry you," said Veronica.

"Who?" Zalem asked.

"My mother," answered Veronica.

"Your mother? I thought your mother was dead," said Zalem.

"I thought she was, too, but somehow she didn't die. She wants me to marry you. Don't you see that I must marry you?" said Veronica as she continued to cry.

"I get why she wants us to be married, but she has no hold on me. I will make sure your father gets out. But we don't need to get married," said Zalem.

"You don't understand, she hurts the ones that you love, Zalem. She forced me to tell her that I kissed Ethan. She told me she wouldn't hurt anyone, but she really did hurt you," said Veronica.

"You are not making any sense, Veronica. She hasn't hurt me," said Zalem, very puzzled.

"I am so sorry, Zalem, please forgive me. I

wanted no part in this. Remember, I want to be with Ethan," said Veronica as she got down on her knees and begged. She cried and begged and dragged his clothing.

"You still haven't explained. Tell me how she has hurt me," said Zalem forcefully.

"Forgive me...She has your grandparents and has threatened everyone else that you love," said Veronica. Zalem pulled away from her in anger. "I am sorry, Prince Zalem," said Veronica. She was on her hands and knees on the floor.

"I don't believe you. My grandparents are at their kingdom. If they weren't, we would have been summoned," said Zalem.

"The other castle thinks they are here, and she wants me to take you to the forest to see them. There she will tell you what to do," said Veronica.

"How do I know this isn't an ambush?" said Zalem.

"She doesn't want to hurt you. She wants us to get married. She gave me this to prove that she has them," said Veronica as she held out their crowns, and his grandmother's necklace that she never took off. Zalem was torn apart in fear on the inside, but on the outside, he was calm, and tried to think on his feet.

"When and where?" asked Zalem.

"We have to sneak out together tonight. No one must know that we are going. I don't want anyone else to be in danger, so please don't tell them. OK?" said Veronica.

"OK, I will just avoid them," said Zalem. He sighed and snuck back to his chambers.

Throughout the day, Zalem tried his hardest to avoid everyone. Isabelle searched for Zalem all day but couldn't find him. She had work to do for Lillianna, so she couldn't concentrate on finding him. While Isabelle was with Lillianna she told her the good news. Isabelle was so excited to talk about her and Zalem finally getting a chance at love. As Isabelle and Lillianna talked about Zalem, he walked by Lillianna's chambers and overheard it all. He was so sad because that's the life he wanted, but feared he would never have. Lillianna thought she heard a noise and went to look, but Zalem had disappeared.

That night, Zalem and Veronica met up again and now had to sneak out of the castle into the forest. They snuck by the Queen, Lathem, and many guards, and finally got into the forest. They both thought that they were home free, not knowing that Lillianna had seen them both enter the forest. Lillianna was looking out of the dining room, sitting by the windowsill. Lillianna didn't understand what they were doing together, and she was so upset. She couldn't stand for this anymore.

Zalem and Veronica had gone pretty far into the forest when Zalem asked, "How much further do we have to go?"
"Not far; two men are supposed to meet us at the clearing," said Veronica. All of a sudden, two men dropped down from the trees and knocked them unconscious. When Zalem awoke, he was chained to a chair, staring at his grandparents behind bars. He turned and saw Veronica unconscious and her father, King Maxwell, behind bars as well. Her father, and his grandmother and

grandfather, were separately caged. Out walked a woman with two guards. She told one man to remove the cloth that she had rolled and tied across Zalem's mouth, across his cheeks, and that knotted behind his nape.

As soon as the man removed it, Zalem said, "How dare you? Let us go. I came to you unarmed just to see my family and to hear what you want me to do."

Veronica then woke up, and her mother told one of the guards to take the cloth off her mouth. Then her mother began to speak.

"Hello. It's great to see the two of you. I brought you both here to explain what I want you to do." She smiled.

"And what is that, get married? We already know that," said Zalem.

"I didn't interrupt you, so please, don't interrupt me. But yes, I want the two of you married. You cannot tell anyone about me, or our deal, or else the deal is done and they will all die. Everyone must believe that the both of you are in love," said Veronica's mother in a calm manner. She then pointed to Zalem and said, "I want you to dump any other girl in the way, and I want you, Veronica, to get Ethan out of your head. The both of you will go home and plan a wedding. Don't think that these three are the only ones in danger. Your father could get hurt, or Lillianna and that baby. That would be tragic." Zalem got mad and wanted to attack her, but he was tied up.

And then she turned to Veronica and said, "Or even Ethan, he is such a cute boy." She smirked.

"You promised you wouldn't hurt him," said Veronica.

"You're right. I did say that, but I didn't promise that I wouldn't separate the two of you. I could send him away. Are we clear, the both of you?" asked her mother.

They both nodded their heads "yes," and Veronica decided to ask her mother a question. "Why do you want us married so badly?"

Her mother answered, "That's a good question. I want you to be the most powerful queen ever."

Zalem didn't believe that lie at all, but he just went with it. Zalem decided to check on his grandparents. He asked them, "How are the two of you?"

His grandfather answered, "We're OK."

"I am so sorry that this is happening to you," said his grandmother.

"No," said Zalem as he shook his head and continued, "I am so sorry that the both of you are even involved in my problems."

"This is not a bad thing, this is a good thing. Why are you people making it sound so bad?" said Veronica's mother.

"It is a bad thing, and please, don't interrupt me," said Zalem as he turned back and began to speak to his grandparents again. "I promise to get you out of here as soon as I can. I love both of you."

"We love you, too," said his grandfather.

"Yes, we do. We love you so much," said his grandmother. She began to cry.

While Zalem was talking to his grandparents, Veronica was talking to her father. "Father, I am so sorry about this," said Veronica. She realized her father's mouth had a cloth over it so he could not speak. "Why is there a cloth over his face? I came all this way to see him," demanded Veronica.

"Yes, you came to see him, not speak to him. You're lucky he is even alive," said her mother in an aggressive voice.

Veronica wanted to cry, but she held it in. She didn't want her mother to see that she was weak, so she held it in and began to talk to her father. "I know you can't respond, and I know you love me, and I love you. I promise to get you out of here" she said.

"OK, that's enough talking. The both of you need to get working on this wedding," said her mother as she told the guards to help them up. They both were blindfolded, and their mouths covered once again. Then they were carried back to the forest, where they would be picked up. The two men dropped them both on the ground and cut the rope off of Veronica's hands, unchained Zalem's hands, then ran off. Zalem took off the blindfolds to try and see where the men had run to, but they were gone.

He then took off the mouth covering and the rope around his feet. So did Veronica, but she moved a little slower than Zalem, so he helped her remove the rope from her feet. They both stood up and began their walk back to the castle. The lantern they had been using was still there, but unlit. So Zalem took two rocks and lit it again. As they walked back, Veronica was silent almost all the way there. Zalem, too, was quiet the entire time. Finally, Veronica said "I can't believe we have to do this." Zalem ignored her.

They finally reached the castle and Zalem decided to speak. "I will make sure that everyone believes we're together. I will propose to you today, but for now let's sneak back to our chambers and get a little sleep. Then we'll gather the family," he said. Veronica agreed, and they went their separate ways.

Veronica snuck all the way back to her chambers unseen. Zalem got all the way to his chambers and was about to walk in, when he heard someone call his name.

Zalem turned around and saw Lillianna there. "It's very late, Lillianna. You should be asleep. Why are you awake? Is the baby OK?" he asked.

"Yes, the baby and I are OK. I was worried about you," said Lillianna.

"Don't worry about me, Lillianna. I am OK, as long as the ones I love are OK. Go back to bed" said Zalem.

"I can't, Zalem. If you care for the ones you love, then please don't lie. Tell me why you went to the forest with Veronica," said Lillianna.

Zalem grabbed Lillianna and brought her into the chambers and shut the door. "You saw that?" said Zalem.

"Yes, I did, and how dare you tell Isabelle that you want to be with her and then run off with Veronica," she said angrily.

"How did you know?" said Zalem. He paused, and then realized that Isabelle told Lillianna because they were best friends. "I didn't know Isabelle told you," said Zalem.

"Yes, she did, and I am so ashamed of you," said Lillianna even more angrily.

Zalem wanted to tell Lillianna the entire truth, but he remembered what Veronica's mother had told him. "I am sorry that Isabelle got that impression, but I want Veronica. I am in love with her. That's the truth," said Zalem.

Lillianna was in shock, and couldn't believe that any of this was true. "You're lying," she said.

"No, I am not. Please Lillianna, just go back to sleep. I am tired and I have a lot to announce to our family tomorrow," said Zalem as he held the door open.

Lillianna shook her head and began to walk out. She said, "I don't know what's going on, but I can see in your eyes that you're not happy with this decision."

"I am fine, and I know what I have decided. Goodnight," said Zalem as he let her out, then shut the door. He hated himself for lying to Lillianna, but he had to lie to Isabelle, as well. Tomorrow would be a big day, so Zalem tried to sleep but had no luck. Veronica tried as well, and had so many nightmares that she just lay awake, all night.

While Zalem and Veronica both lay awake dazed, Veronica's mother was telling the guards to remove the cloth from King Maxwell's mouth. She dismissed the guards and began to speak to him. Zalem's grandparents were sleeping, or they appeared to be.

"Malinda, why are you so evil? You wouldn't even let me speak to my daughter," said King Maxwell.

"You mean our daughter, Maxwell," said Malinda.

"No, I mean my daughter. We both know she isn't truly yours. You were supposed to be a better mother than her mother. Her mother walked out on us. I just didn't want her to grow up motherless, and look at what you're doing to her," said King Maxwell.

"Are you done talking, Maxwell? That little girl is as much mine as yours," said Malinda.

"Why did you want to become her mother, if you were going to treat her like this? Now she will hate you," said King Maxwell.

"If you would finally stop talking, I would get

to explain. I don't really care for the girl. I just hated her mother, and made sure her mother was sent away," said Malinda.

"Sent away? After all these years, now you tell me this. Why, why would you do this?" said King Maxwell.

"I did all of this to tear apart your family and get rid of everyone who would be in the way of my taking over the kingdom. When Veronica becomes queen and you're dead, I will force her to give me the kingdom. I want her to have nothing, just like I do," said Malinda.

"I get that you want the kingdom, but why destroy my family?" asked King Maxwell.

"My family was destroyed by her mother, and she destroyed other families as well. She isn't here to stand up for her mistakes, so Veronica will pay," said Malinda.

"As long as I am alive I will protect her," said Maxwell.

"I know you will, but that's why soon you will die. You should be happy I am allowing her to live," said Malinda. Maxwell didn't answer her, and rolled over. "Anyway, I have to be going to sleep. There is so much planning for me to do to get ready to take over the kingdom. Goodnight," said Malinda. Maxwell stopped her and asked, "Why did you play dead?"

Malinda replied, "To put all of this into effect. I needed time. You and Veronica just kept on getting in the way." She left and went off to bed.

Chapter 12

The next day, Zalem and Veronica awoke very stressed out. They both knew what they had to do, but continued to feel bad. Zalem dressed and told Sir Luther about getting everyone into the ballroom for an announcement. Within half an hour they were all there.

Zalem then began to speak. "I thank all of you for coming here on such a beautiful day, but I have an announcement to make. I have chosen a bride." Everyone clapped. Isabelle was so happy, and she couldn't wait for him to call her name. She was in shock, because she wasn't expecting this. "I want to present my bride to everyone. Can you please come forward, Princess Veronica?" said Zalem as everyone began to clap again.

Isabelle stepped back into the crowd, while Veronica stepped forward, smiling. Lillianna felt so bad for Isabelle, and she was mad at Zalem for embarrassing Isabelle like that. "Veronica, from the first day I met you, I knew you were special, but I never thought it would become love. You will be a great queen as well," said Zalem as he got down on one knee. "Veronica, you're the best thing that has happened to me in a long time." He pulled out a box that had his grandmother's ring in it. Then he said, "Will you marry me?" Veronica played the part well and accepted the ring, while Isabelle looked like she was about to throw up. Isabelle backed out of the room. Only Lillianna saw, and began to go after her, but not before looking at Zalem very disappointedly. Zalem and Veronica were now engaged. "I don't want to wait, so I would want us to be married by tomorrow morning," he said.

As Isabelle walked out the door, she heard the wedding date and couldn't believe it.

Isabelle's heart was broken. She found a chair in the hall and broke down crying. Lillianna grabbed her as Isabelle asked, "Why couldn't he tell me instead of making me stand through that? I don't get it." Lillianna responded, "I don't know why," as Lillianna held her in her arms and Isabelle began to cry.

Veronica had a lot to do to prepare for a wedding, so she and Zalem went their separate ways to get measured for their wedding clothes. The castle was in utter chaos. Flowers had to be chosen and picked out of the garden, because there was no time for any exports. The hairstyles, bridesmaids, maid of honor, groomsmen, best man, rings, and more all had to be chosen. Queen Tianna grew worried about Zalem and was wondering if he was rushing into something he wasn't ready for. She decided to wait until he wasn't that busy to talk to him. Lillianna was so upset that she wasn't waiting and went directly to him. Zalem went in for his measurements, and Lillianna barged in. She began to yell at Zalem. "How dare you embarrass Isabelle? I know she may not be special to you, but she is more than just a servant. She has feelings, Zalem, and I am not cleaning up your messes anymore. You owe her an explanation."

He replied, "You're right. I was wrong and I should have talked to her, but I have so much to do and I have no time for anything else."

Lillianna got even more upset and yelled, "What's wrong with you, Zalem? It's like you've become a new person. I don't even know who you are."

He replied, "I am sorry you feel that way, but I have a lot to do. Just go and relax."

Lillianna replied, "I am ashamed of the person you have become," as she began to feel a pain in her abdomen. She held her belly and squealed, but by the time the pain stopped she was surrounded by everyone, even Zalem. She ended up being taken into her chambers, where her doctor came to check on her. The doctor put Lillianna on bed rest until the baby was born.

Zalem was so upset, but decided to put his

feelings aside. He felt like what happened to Lillianna was his fault. Even though it happened, Zalem had a wedding to plan. Before he left the her chambers where Lillianna was being checked out, Queen Tianna whispered in his ear. "Can we meet later in the library?" He nodded and they continued on. Everything went back to normal, except Isabelle wouldn't leave Lillianna's side.

That night after dinner, Zalem met with Queen Tianna. They both went and sat down on a couch. "I don't expect to talk that long, because I know you have a big day tomorrow," said Queen Tianna.
Zalem said, "Yeah, I do, but why did you call me here?"
She replied, "I wanted to ask you if you're sure this is what you want."
Zalem sighed, then said, "I've known since I met her that I wanted her to be my wife."
The Queen replied, "OK. If so, then why are you rushing things? Why get married so quickly?"
Zalem responded, "I can't go another

moment without her. I have been waiting way too long, and I want to begin my life." Then he sighed and looked down and asked, "How did you know you wanted to get married to my father?"

The Queen replied, "I was scared to marry your dad. Remember, I was supposed to tell you the story of how we met. If you want to know, I can tell you now."

Zalem agreed quickly, because he was eager to hear. The Queen then began to explain. "All right then. When your mother passed away, your father was heartbroken and I didn't believe he would ever love again. I was always there, but as a friend. Well, I was a worker in the palace—that's probably why I am so nice to the workers and servants. I worked in the kitchen. We played together as kids, even though the royal family hated when we were together."

Zalem asked, "Why didn't they want that?"

The Queen began to explain again, "The royal family felt that it was pointless for us to be together, because I could never become his wife or royalty. They also thought I had nothing to offer to him."

Zalem then interrupted again and said, "The way Lillianna is with Isabelle, and you with Rose, I would have never guessed. When my father explained his father, I got the impression that he was strict. He wouldn't let him marry who he wanted."

The Queen replied, "That's correct, but he loved your mother. He decided to do what he wanted after she passed away. He realized that life was too short. It took him a while to date, and then later we married and had Lillianna. When I worked in the kitchen, I thought nothing more of it, but your father fell in love with me. I am grateful that he did, and I love him dearly. Zalem, I hope this story helps you, but I want to tell you something else." Zalem looked and she began to talk again. "When I was a young girl, I found Ramina outside the palace and I was the one that invited her in. She had run away. That's all she said, and she never talked about it, but sometimes I think if I didn't let her in, you would have grown up in the palace. I am sorry for that."

Zalem turned to her and said, "I don't blame you for that at all. Ramina did what she wanted, and there's nothing we can do but look to what comes ahead. I am really grateful that you told me, thank you." He gave her a hug.

"That's great. Well, I am going to bed; you should do the same. It's going to be a big day tomorrow. Goodnight," said the Queen as she got up.

"Goodnight," Zalem said as she walked away, Zalem began to think. He realized that he really wanted Isabelle, and he had to figure out a plan to get his life back. He got up and went to Veronica, as she was walking out of her chambers. They began to whisper.

"What are you doing here, Zalem?" asked Veronica as she grabbed him into the corner.

"You don't want to marry me, right?" asked Zalem.

"You know I don't, but we have to," said Veronica.

"You're right. I don't, either, but I have a plan to save the both of us," said Zalem.

"That's great, Zalem, but how do you know

she won't see straight through it?" said Veronica.

"She won't; it's foolproof. Just tell her that the wedding is on for tomorrow. She should come with your father and my grandparents—either to the wedding, or close by," said Zalem.

"Zalem, I don't know. I just want them safe and unharmed," said Veronica.

"I do as well, but we have to do this. We cannot just do what she wants. Just do as I say, and everything will be OK. Trust me," said Zalem.

Veronica agreed, and she walked into her chambers to prepare to visit her mother. Zalem quickly grabbed Sir Luther. "Yes, sire?" answered Sir Luther.

"I need you to do something very important, but you can't be seen or heard. OK?" asked Zalem, breathing heavily and eagerly.

"Yes, sire," answered Sir Luther.

"I want you to follow Veronica and make sure she walks into and out of where she is going safely. When Veronica leaves, stay there and make sure the woman there brings my grandparents and Veronica's father out to the wedding. They have been kidnapped for ransom. If she brings them, then make sure they are safe traveling back, and follow them. If she does not, then I need you to rescue them. But I beg you to not be seen or heard, because no one is supposed to know, even Veronica."

"Yes, Sire, I will protect them with my life," answered Sir Luther.

"And you be careful as well, Sir Luther. That's an order," said Zalem. Sir Luther bowed. He quickly got some things and ran off and followed Veronica into the forest. She found the guards, who blindfolded her and carried her to her mother. Sir Luther stayed behind. He walked and saw the men go into a shack. He hid in the bushes and waited. Veronica went in and explained everything to her mother. She checked on the three prisoners as well. Her mother told her she'd be at the wedding, but she did not know who would be accompanying her. Veronica then was blindfolded and taken away again. Sir Luther saw her leave, and waited to see what the woman's decision was going to be for the fate of Zalem's grandparents and Veronica's father.

Chapter 13

The big day had finally arrived, even though it was put together in such a hurry. People were moving back and forth through the entire kingdom. Zalem had never seen so many servants move so fast. In the chaos, Zalem was trying to find Veronica but could not.

With the wedding buzzing through the palace and all the guards talking about it, everyone knew, including the prisoners in the dungeon. Sir Adam was talking to Sir Francis about the wedding, as they were delivering prison trays and picking up buckets. Each prisoner was separate from one another. All prisoners were chained, and the chains were long enough to reach to the prisoners' bars. The tray for their food remained on the inside, in front of the bars, with the buckets. There was a small door at the bottom of the bars to fit the bucket in and out, and to put a ladle through to put food on the trays. This happened twice a day.

As they both continued to deliver food, they reached Ramina's cell. Ramina blurted out, "My son is getting married."

Sir Adam answered, "Zalem is getting married today." They continued walking and doing their job, while Ramina came up with a beautiful idea. She just had to be at the wedding.

At the same time, Sir Luther was still outside in the bushes waiting for Veronica's mother to bring out the three captives. Sir Luther was becoming very tired, but just as he was about to fall asleep, he heard the door open. Sir Luther saw two of her guards and a man blindfolded and tied up with them. Sir Luther realized that Zalem's grandparents were still locked up in there.

He had to think of a plan to get them out. He snuck around the other side of the shack, making sure to duck down and avoid the windows. He remained crouched down and leaned against the wall, trying to peek in through the window. But it was blocked by thick, black blinds. Sir Luther found a small crack on another part of the shack. He saw three guards, but he did not see Zalem's grandparents.

He then decided he was either going to sneak in, or fight his way through. Sir Luther only saw one door, so there was no sneaking in. He also did not want to fight, because the men looked much stronger than him. He then quickly thought of a great plan to make a distraction outside. Sir Luther decided to gather up some big branches and make a fire. He made it as high as his waist, but it went along the entire front of the house with just enough room to walk out and see it. He then got two rocks and lit the branches many times.

Afterward, he grabbed a big leaf to make the fire blaze faster. Sir Luther then threw two

rocks at the door, and then he hid. One of
the guards peeked through a hole in the
door that he slid open and then closed.
When he saw the line of fire, he ran out and
called for the other guards to grab some
buckets of water.

When they both ran outside to put the fire
out, Sir Luther then snuck in. When he got
in he remembered that he had seen one
more guard, so he hid behind a barrel. The
third guard heard the guards outside calling
him, so he came up from underground
through a door with a latch. Sir Luther
worked his way through to the door and
snuck in when no one was looking. He
slowly shut the floor board down behind
him.

He saw Zalem's grandparents caged like
dogs. Sir Luther saw that the cells were
locked and searched for keys. He spotted
them on the wall. He quickly grabbed them
and unlocked the cells. Queen Liza was so
grateful that she gave him the biggest hug.
He made sure it was a quick hug, and then
he opened King Edward's cell. Sir Luther

helped him up and looked around the room. He saw a sword next to the barrel and gave it to King Edward to use to protect himself. When he handed him the sword, Sir Luther said, "We are going to have to fight our way out. There are three guards up there. One should be unarmed because you have his sword. Zalem sent me to look out for you; that means if I get injured, just leave and run. I am here for that, and I know I can die."

The Queen responded back, "Honey, I know your heart is loyal, but that is why I cannot leave you." She walked toward him and rubbed his hand. Then they heard footsteps. Sir Luther went in front and told them to follow him. Then Sir Luther barged open the door and began to fight his way out.

King Edward came up with the Queen behind his back. King Edward realized that there was one guard who was unarmed, which made things easier. But he still had to fight two guards at once. All of a sudden, the King killed one guard, and Sir Luther killed another, but the third guard had found himself a knife and had it at the Queen's neck. The guard screamed at them. "Drop your swords, or I'll kill her."

They both dropped their swords, and the guard began to back away toward the door. Sir Luther had to think quickly. He grabbed the knife and the two of them began to fight over it. The Queen ran into her husband's arms, and he pushed her behind him. But before King Edward could kill the guard, the guard stabbed Sir Luther in the torso. Then the King killed the guard, and the Queen ran to Sir Luther and pulled the knife out. She quickly tended to his wound, while he begged them to leave. The Queen ignored him, and when she was done cleaning his wound and fixing it, she and the King carried him back to the castle.

While they headed to the castle, the wedding was about to begin. Lillianna could not attend the wedding, so Isabelle and Royal stayed with her while Zion attended. Everyone was there and seated in the royal ballroom, awaiting their new queen. The royal ballroom looked beautiful for something so quickly put together. As Zalem walked in, he smelled the aroma of the tulips. Everything was pink and white. Hanging from the ceiling were drapes that were white and lined with gold and pink tulips. The four drapes hung from the four corners of the ceiling and met at the top of the chandelier. The altar was lined with tulips, and the bride and groom were to stand underneath a flower arch. The walls had candle holders and pink and white drapes that hung from the giant, glassless window. The room was stunning, but that wasn't Zalem's concern.

Zalem walked up to the front and looked around for his grandparents and Veronica's father, but he didn't see them. Veronica, on the other hand, was pacing the floor nervously in her chambers, when her mother walked in with her father. "You look so beautiful," said her mother as she began to touch Veronica's curls. Veronica gracefully took her hand off, but she really wanted to slap her.

"My lady, sir, guests should be in the

ballroom," said a servant as she bowed. "Yes, I guess I should be, but remember what we talked about, Veronica," said her mother as she winked and walked out. Veronica hugged her father. He knew he couldn't tell Veronica anything, because there was a guard outside the door who would kill Veronica, Zalem's grandparents, and anyone else who stood in Malinda's way.

Down in the ballroom, Zalem saw King Maxwell walk in with a woman, but her face was covered with a red birdcage blusher lace veil. He assumed it was Veronica's mother. He became uneasy, wondering where his grandparents were. The wedding then began, and everyone was asked to be seated. Zalem's best man was Zion, and they stood at the alter waiting. King Joseph was officiating the ceremony. King Joseph told them all to rise as Princess Veronica walked down the aisle in a gorgeous white dress with a long train. The dress was big and poufy below the waist, but at the top, it hugged her torso and was encrusted with gold. It was sleeveless, and the bottom of the dress was lined with a gold design. Her shoes were white with a gold bow buckle with diamonds at each outer ankle. Her veil was a mantilla elbow-length veil with a gold hair comb attached to it that had diamonds in it. Her veil was lined in white with a thick, gold line above the white line, all along the veil.

She finally got to the altar, and Zalem whispered to her, "Where are my grandparents?" They turned and walked up two steps to King Joseph.

"Maybe at a shack nearby," she answered quickly, so nobody could hear them, with a smile on her face.

King Joseph smiled down at them and began to speak. "We come here today to bring my son Zalem and the woman he loves together before God. I want to get the hard part out of the way before we continue, because you know it can really mess up a wedding." Everyone laughed, and he continued, "If there is a reason that this man and this woman should not be wed, speak now or forever hold your piece."

Everyone looked around, and then all of a sudden, Ramina burst in and ran down the aisle. Zalem's jaw almost hit the floor.

"Zalem, how could you get married and not tell your mother?" screamed Ramina.

King Joseph then loudly said, "Guards, guards."

"You're not my mother," answered Zalem as he approached her. He said, "You knew my mother died, and you never told me."

Ramina answered, "But I raised you and gave you the love and care and..."

Zalem interrupted her, yelling, "No, you took my life from me and my family and that's something I would never forgive you for. Guards, take her away."

As she was turned around by the guards, King Maxwell noticed her face and yelled out, "Julianna, wait, Julianna. Is it really you, Julianna?"

While he ran to her, Zalem yelled out, "Guards, guards," and told them to halt.

King Maxwell was so excited to see her. He said, "You came back to me. How? I thought you were dead."

She replied, "I wasn't. I ran away, but I see that you married again."

King Maxwell replied, "No, you don't understand. I thought you were dead, and I married again so my beautiful...well, our beautiful daughter wouldn't grow up without a mother."

Veronica walked down off the platform and asked, "Father, what are you trying to say?" He grabbed his daughter's hands with his and held onto them firmly, then he guided her in front of him and said, "Oh, Veronica, please don't be mad at me. Malinda isn't your mother, Julianna is."

Julianna asked, "That is the baby I left years ago?" She began to cry.

"Why did you leave?" asked King Maxwell. Before he could get an answer, Veronica interrupted and yelled at Malinda, "You evil witch, you knew this entire time and made me believe this lie." Malinda unveiled herself and everyone saw her face.

Julianna quickly recognized her, and asked, "Ilianna, is that you?" She looked at her, pondering.

"Yes, it is," Malinda answered.

"Ilianna? I thought your name was Malinda. How do you know each other?" asked Veronica.

"She is my sister. And yes, my real name is Ilianna."

"Well, she is my wife," answered King Maxwell as he pointed to Ilianna.

Julianna was full of anger and rage, and began to yell and pull away from the guards.

"How dare you marry the man I loved, Ilianna?" yelled Julianna.

"Well, if you loved him so much, why did you leave them?" asked Ilianna.

"Don't act like you don't know why, Ilianna. I left because you told me that he didn't love me, and that he loved another. So I had to leave because you assured me they would kill me." Julianna then turned to King Maxwell and continued, "When I heard you married again, it broke my heart. That made me really believe that everything was true." The King had an epiphany, and said to Ilianna, "That's why you came along very eager to make sure Veronica had a mother."

Julianna then asked, "Why did you do this to me?"

Ilianna responded, "You were too young and dumb, and I was the older sister that could not bear children."

Julianna replied, "But why hurt me like that? I wanted to be a mother so badly that I stole Zalem from his own family. I can't believe I did exactly what you did. You told me I was too young to be a mother, and that I would screw it up, so I ran off and you told them that I died." She broke down crying and said, "You told me I was a miller's daughter, and that I was crazy to think a king would ever love me, even though my father was a lord. You even said that you overheard them saying they were going to kill me," said Julianna.

"You deserve everything that comes to you," said Ilianna.

"Guards, seize that woman," Zalem instructed loudly, pointing at Ilianna. She turned to Zalem and shook her head, and said, "Oh, Zalem, you don't want to do that. You do want to see your grandparents again.

If I don't return, they will be killed."

At that moment, Sir Adam walked through the door and gave Zalem a look of assurance that they were OK. Then Zalem yelled, "Take her away."

Ilianna responded, "Zalem, if you do this, then you'll never know how your mother truly died." She spoke calmly, but loud enough for him to hear.

"Wait, guards," said Zalem as he grabbed Ilianna. He screamed, "If you know something, then tell me." He tossed her to the ground.

Ilianna laughed vengefully and said, "You stupid boy, I snuck into the palace and mixed the drink with poison that killed her." The entire room became unsettled and Zalem asked, "What did you say?"

Ilianna responded, "You heard me. I mixed it, but someone else delivered it to her." She spoke in a taunting voice.

"Who was it? I'll have their head for this!" screamed King Joseph.

"The person is in this room," said Ilianna.

"Guards, lock the doors. I don't want them to

leave," King Joseph commanded.

Zalem turned to Ilianna and asked, "Who was it?"

She turned to King Joseph and laughed, then said, "It was your beloved wife, Queen Tianna." The entire room looked at her and the Queen was silent.

"No, that is not true. Lock her up!" screamed Zalem as he pointed to Ilianna but stared at Tianna for an answer.

The King turned to his wife and asked her, "Is it true?"

She looked at the King, and he knew it was true. She then blurted out, "I didn't know what it was; I was just told to give it to her. I had no idea that I killed her." Queen Tianna cried.

As Ilianna was dragged out, she laughed hysterically, saying, "It should have been you, too, Zalem, she just drank it too late. If she drank it before you were born, you would have been dead, too."

At that moment the wedding was over. Sir Adam walked up to Zalem and told him that his grandparents were safe, and that Sir

Luther was injured but going to be OK. Zalem nodded his head yes in assurance. Zion then began to speak. "I apologize to everyone for the confusion, but there will not be a wedding today." Zalem, Veronica, King Maxwell, Julianna, King Joseph, and Queen Tianna were very still, and stuck in a daze. None of them could believe what had happened. Zion continued, and said to the guests, "Please, everyone, go and enjoy the reception food." Everyone got up and left. Veronica went to go and change out of her dress, but she hugged Zalem and gave him the ring before she left. Zalem went to check on Sir Luther. There was so much going on in everyone's minds.

Chapter 14

Later that night, Zalem went to Lillianna's chambers still in his wedding clothes. He wanted to talk to her about his day. He knocked on the door and Zion answered. "She's sleeping," he said.

Zalem replied, "That's OK. I'll wait for her to wake up. You go and eat something, please." Zion agreed, and Zalem went in quietly and sat down by her bedside. He waited for her to awake, just like she always did for him. In about half an hour she awoke, and said, "Zalem, what are you doing here?"

Zalem responded, "Waiting for you to wake up." He laughed. Lillianna smiled as well, and then Zalem spoke again. "Never thought

I'd be by your bedside, huh?" They both laughed again.

"Zion told me everything. I am so sorry," said Lillianna.

"You know what the crazy part is?" asked Zalem.

"What?" Lillianna asked.

"I can actually say that I feel sorry for Ramina, or Julianna, or whoever, and I understand why she took me. She was hurting. I am still upset, but I have calmed down," said Zalem.

"Wow, I'm so mad I missed all of that," said Lillianna.

Zalem burst out laughing, and said, "After all that I said, that's what you're mad about. You're crazy. I wish I wasn't there to see it, or even live it."

"So, what are you going to do about Isabelle?" Lillianna asked, as she got more comfortable in her bed.

"I don't know. Do you think she still wants me?" asked Zalem.

"Yes, Zalem, but you have to go to her," said Lillianna.

At that moment, Isabelle and Zion walked in with food for Lillianna. The laughter from Zion and Isabelle as they walked in turned to silence when Isabelle saw Zalem sitting there. Isabelle gave Lillianna her tray and helped her get even more comfortable. Lillianna then gave Zalem a look saying, *go with her and talk.* Zalem got up, and Isabelle cut him off before he could speak. "Do you need anything else my lady?" she asked, as she turned to receive an answer.

"No, but thank you for asking, Isabelle. You may go," replied Lillianna.

She then turned to leave, and Zalem quickly followed her and began to speak. "Isabelle, Isabelle, Isabelle, please turn around."

He grabbed her arm, and she screamed, "Zalem, what could you possibly want after how you humiliated me? And now you're not even married." She looked disappointed.

"Just hear me out," said Zalem.

"No, I'm done," said Isabelle.

He ran in front of her and tried to stop her. "Please hear me out, and after you do, you never have to hear my voice again. Just please let me explain everything, and I promise to be honest," said Zalem.

Isabelle nodded her head in agreement. They both sat down in chairs in the hall, and began a discussion. "Let me talk, and when I am done, you can yell at me. Deal?" said Zalem. Isabelle nodded again. He started from the night he confessed his feelings to her, and finished at what happened at the wedding. Throughout the conversation, Zalem saw that Isabelle's face had changed. "Now, tell me if you ever want to speak to me again," said Zalem when he was done and he looked down.

Isabelle looked at him and grabbed his face with both hands on his cheeks. Then their eyes met, and she quietly said, "There was nothing to forgive." Tears rolled down their cheeks, and they kissed.

"I love you, Isabelle, and I always have. You don't know how hard it was for me to do what I did. I want you to be my wife and the person I tell my secrets to, and wake up to in the morning. You were always the one. I am sorry that it didn't happen the way you imagined it, but I hope to make sure I work every day to make it better. Just please give me the chance," said Zalem.

She replied back very lovingly, "I wouldn't have it any other way."

Zalem then asked, "Since that is how you feel, I want to do something special for you tonight. Can we meet? I'll be having a small royal ball at eight o'clock, can you be there?"

Isabelle responded, "Yes." They were both so excited.

While Zalem and Isabelle were talking, there was another conversation going on. King Maxwell, Julianna, and Veronica were having a discussion in the foyer. King Maxwell began to speak. "Julianna, I have missed you so much." He gave her a hug.

"I am sorry this happened to us, but I want to get to know you, Veronica," said Julianna.

"I do too, but...," said Veronica. She paused, looking worried.

King Maxwell said, "What is it, Veronica?"

"You can tell us," her mother insisted.

"I do not wish to return home; I wish to follow my heart," said Veronica.

Julianna was sad, but she understood. "I understand, and I wish you all the best. Just promise that you'll visit and we'll get to know each other." She looked toward Veronica for love.

"Yes...Mother," answered Veronica.

"I honestly am sorry, darling. If only I had known better, I would not have left you two. I was young." Julianna began to cry, and Veronica hugged her.

"OK. Since you're fine, Mother...Father, what do you think? I do not want to take the throne," said Veronica, looking at her father.

"Why, Veronica, I worked so hard to make this possible for you," said King Maxwell.

"I know, but please, trust me. I will have money, but I need my true love, and I know the man I want to be with," said Veronica. It was hard for King Maxwell to accept, but he did, and he decided to let her go. Veronica said her good-byes, and she went to talk to Zalem. He told her where to locate her true love and gave her a horse and carriage. Veronica didn't care for the carriage and just took the horse.

When she arrived, Ethan was shocked to see her, and to see that she was unmarried. She ran up to Ethan and told him she loved him and kissed him. Ethan thought he was dreaming, but when reality finally sank in, they became a beautiful couple. When Veronica left, King Maxwell and Julianna decided to return back to their kingdom of Euselus and got remarried.

That same night, King Joseph decided to go down to the dungeon to see Ilianna and ask her a few questions. "Fancy seeing you here," said Ilianna as she laughed.
He brushed off what she said. "I want to know why you killed my late wife and gave Tianna the glass," said the King.
"Haven't you been listening? I could not bear children," said Ilianna.
"Yeah, I heard you say that, but what does that have to do with anything?" said the King.
"Temper, temper! Relax. You asked me a question, and all I am trying to do is answer it. Well, I couldn't bear children because your father cursed me. I wanted to take

away his children, but it didn't work. So I took your mother's life, but that didn't hurt him. Then I took your wife's life, and that didn't hurt him. So I was going to take your child's life, but I couldn't find him, so I ended your father's life," said Ilianna.

"I see that you knew Zalem was alive way before we did; but why didn't you hurt *me*?" said the King.

"The only reason you're alive was so I could get what I wanted. I was going to marry you, but you went off and married Tianna so quickly," answered Ilianna.

"Why did you give the glass to Tianna?" asked the King.

"I did not plan on her being your wife. I just thought that it would be great if your best friend killed your wife. You can't blame me for everything you married the tramp," said Ilianna.

The King then called for a guard. "This woman is mad, and I want her killed by morning," said the King to the guard.

"This is not going to be the last time you see me," said Ilianna, laughing.

"Oh, yes, it will be," said The King.

While the king was with Ilianna, the ballroom was being set up with just two chairs and a beautifully decorated table. There was champagne, and beautiful orchids that decorated the table. All the eating utensils were set up in their right order. Isabelle walked in, looking more beautiful than ever. She was escorted to her seat by Zalem, and then he pushed in her chair and sat down.

"Wow, you really know how to treat a girl," said Isabelle, and they both laughed.

"Thank you for being here. I really need great people in my life," said Zalem. The food came out and they ate and laughed, and then the dessert came, and they ate again and drank, too.

"Zalem, I am having so much fun. I haven't had this much fun in a very long time," said Isabelle.

"Me neither. But I wanted to ask you something, if it isn't too forward," said Zalem.

"Ask me anything," Isabelle said in a very

sweet voice.

Zalem began speaking. "I don't know what I would do without you...You're sweet, kind, and honest. I love the way you laugh; especially the way you walk and talk. It drives me crazy. I watch you all the time when you play with your bracelet. I don't know what you would do without it. I guess what I'm trying to say is that I love you, and I can't be without you." Zalem then pushed out his chair, and went onto the right side of the table in front of Isabelle on one knee and said, "Will you marry me?"

Isabelle was so overwhelmed that she began to cry.

"Don't cry, Izzy, you'll make me cry. What do you say?"

She nodded her head up and down and then said, "Yes, I'll marry you," as he gave her the ring. They then hugged and kissed, and were overjoyed. They couldn't believe that life could be so good for them.

The next day, Sir Luther was named a Duke. His old surname was removed, and he gained a new surname: Zaru. Afterward, the guards got ready to take Ilianna to her beheading. The king awoke early to watch, but when the guards went down to her cell she was gone.

The entire palace was searched, but she couldn't be found. They even searched the entire kingdom, but she couldn't be found. Ilianna had vanished, and King Joseph was worried all over again.

Chapter 15

Four and a half months later, in late
February, Lillianna, Zion, King Joseph,
Queen Tianna, Zalem, Isabelle, and Royal
were sitting around the fireplace. Lillianna
had a new caretaker, named Tammie, who
stayed by her side because Lillianna was not
to be up and moving too much until the
baby was born. Lillianna was overdue and
tired of being pregnant.

While they were all sitting, King Joseph
decided to sing while everyone else either
drank tea or hot cocoa. When Sir Francis
came in with news from the kingdom of
Euselus, everyone quickly became silent and
gave their attention to him. He then began to

say, "King Maxwell has sent a scroll saying that he and Queen Julianna will be expecting a baby." They all were excited and began to cheer, and Sir Francis headed back out of the room.

When Lillianna took a sip of hot cocoa and then felt some pain in her lower abdomen, she dropped the cup on the floor. Zion and Zalem ran to her side and everyone else stood up. "Lillianna," Zion shouted. "Are you OK?"

"Honey," said the Queen.

"Lill," said Zalem.

"Umm...yeah...I'm OK, but my water broke," said Lillianna.

"OK, Isabelle, get the doctor," said Zion.

"Tammie, get hot water boiling, and Joseph, please get someone to prepare her bed," said the Queen.

Zalem grabbed Royal and took care of him. Everyone ran quickly to get everything put together. Zion lifted Lillianna to the health chambers, as her mother followed. He laid her down in her bed and the doctor ran in, with Tammie and the hot water. Tammie was immediately instructed by the doctor to bring towels and other supplies. The Queen shut the door directly after Tammie walked out. The King and Zalem remained outside the door, pacing the floor. The Queen, Isabelle, and Zion stayed inside. Outside the door, Zalem and the King heard many screams of pain from Lillianna. They both were so worried, but beyond the door, inside of her chambers, Lillianna had begun to push. Zion held her hand, while her mother and Isabelle held her legs. Tammie waited with a blanket for the baby. The doctor instructed her to begin to push, while everyone else in the room began to coach Lillianna on.

Lillianna finally delivered a beautiful baby girl. She named her Lilly, for her favorite flower. The doctor handed the baby to Tammie, and Tammie showed the baby to Lillianna, and then went to clean her off. Everyone was so excited. The King and Zalem finally began to relax, and came into the room.

Lillianna was smiling and so happy, but then

she felt a pain in her abdomen. "Doctor, am I still supposed to be feeling pain and an urge to push?" asked Lillianna. The doctor quickly ran and looked under the blanket, and saw another baby with its legs sticking out.

The doctor replied hastily, "Lillianna, stop. Don't push. Don't do anything." Everyone was worried, wondering what was going on. "Lillianna, you have a breached baby. I need to take her out carefully, or she will die. So please, even if you have the urge to push, don't."

Lillianna wanted to cry because the pain was intense. Zion held her hand and gave her a kiss, while her mother rubbed her head. Isabelle ran and got more blankets for the next baby. The doctor finally got the baby out. She was still and quiet. "Why isn't she crying?" yelled Zalem.

"Wait, give me a minute," said the doctor, as he patted her on the butt. Isabelle walked back in the room with the blankets, and they all heard the baby cry. Isabelle held out the blanket and the doctor wrapped the baby up and held her in his arms. He walked over to Lillianna and said, "This baby is very special; she was also tangled in the umbilical cord. Give her a special name because she is a miracle, and very tiny. She almost didn't make it."

Lillianna smiled and cried as she held her, and said to her, "I love you more than you know."

Everyone smiled, and the King asked, "So what are you going to name her?"

Lillianna looked at Zion to see if he had any ideas, and he replied, "I have no idea."

Zalem said, "I have an idea."

Lillianna replied, "Really? Come here, Zalem." She held out her hand for him to come closer, and in the other hand she held the baby. He came, then she asked, "What is it?"

He replied, "Well, I have been reading a little on our grandmother, our father's mother, and her name was Lila, which means creation. And she is a beautiful creation."

Lillianna looked at him and began to cry.

"What's wrong Lillianna, did I say something

wrong?" asked Zalem as he gave her a hug. Lillianna handed the baby to Isabelle to get cleaned off. She then replied, "No, you didn't say anything wrong. I really love the name, and I think it's great. What do you think, Zion?"

Zion replied, "I think it's great. Thanks, Zalem."

The King said, "Yeah, thanks, Zalem," as he placed his hand on Zalem's shoulder. The Queen even nodded her head in agreement, with tears in her eyes.

Those two beautiful girls added so much joy to the palace. They went from crawling to running, to trying new foods and crying the night away. Everyone played a big part in the children's lives. They all played with the babies and went through all the rough patches, including the good, the bad, or the ugly.

During that time Zalem and Isabelle continued to date, and they decided on a wedding date. They both didn't want to rush things, so they decide to wait. Isabelle didn't want to rush because she wanted to get to know Zalem, and Zalem didn't want to rush because he wanted to let Isabelle plan the wedding of her dreams. They decided to have a grand wedding. They chose to have the wedding the following year, in March, when the girls were both a year old, so they could be the flower girls. They also needed a ring bearer, and he was Victor, King Maxwell and Queen Julianna's son, who was now eight months old.

Their wedding was held inside, and the colors were white and midnight blue, because it was Isabelle's favorite color. Their theme was winter frost. Even though it was late winter, there was still snow on the ground. Zalem couldn't wait to get married, but Isabelle was so nervous. She really didn't want anything to go wrong.

After all the planning had finally been done, it was the day that they had been waiting for. Isabelle and her mother were getting ready, and the Queen, Lillianna, Lila, Lilly, and Royal were all there helping her. Tammie took care of Isabelle's hair and makeup. Isabelle, for once, was perfectly fine and couldn't wait to get married, but her other half, Zalem, wasn't.

Zalem decided to go to the library, where he was looking into his family history. For some reason, he was really interested in his grandmother Lila. King Joseph was looking for him, and finally found him sitting down reading in the library. The King approached him and said, "I thought I was never going to find you so interested in our family history." Zalem replied, "I guess, but it's nothing," as he closed the book and placed it on the table.

The King said, "I wanted to give you something." He pulled out the end of the chain that he always kept tucked into his shirt. The King continued to speak, "I always wear this chain, because it keeps a piece of my past tucked away." He held it out for Zalem to see and continued, "It was a piece of your mother's necklace." The King gave it to Zalem.

He held it closely and examined it, and then asked, "How did you get this?"

The King responded, "It was three days

before your mother passed away. I was preparing to leave, and come back before you were born. Your mother and I were having an argument."

Zalem interrupted, "An argument? What about?"

King Joseph answered, "Yes, an argument. Even as amazing as your mother was, we were married and we argued. We were arguing over my leaving. She knew I had to leave, but she didn't want me to go."

Zalem interrupted again, "Why did you leave?"

The King responded, "I left because I had gotten a letter that said that your grandfather was in danger, and that I would find him at the Kingdom of Euselus. Your mother thought it was a trap. If I had known it was, she wouldn't have been killed."

As the king continued, his eyes began to fill with tears, and Zalem said, "Father, you didn't know. But how did you get the piece?"

The King answered, "Ah yes, the piece...Your mother had a necklace with her name on it, and when she was yelling, I tried to grab her face, and my ring got caught in her necklace. When it broke, your mother and I went to pick up the piece, and she began to laugh and said, 'Look at us. We look so foolish arguing.' I laughed, too, and she told me to hold on to the piece that broke until I returned. I have the E.L.I. and she holds the Z.A. in her grave. Believe me, Zalem, if I had known it was her they were after, I would have stayed and been a better husband. I would have protected my wife and you, too, Zalem."

Zalem stood up and gave his father a hug. Then he said, "You're an amazing father, and I would never ask for anyone else but you." When the hug broke, the king held both of Zalem's forearms and said, "Zalem, I guess I'm saying all this because today is your wedding, and you must protect your wife and the family that is to come. Please be better than me."

Zalem looked away, and the king gripped him a little harder and said, "Promise me." Zalem nodded his head in agreement.

He then said, "OK, Father, let's get ourselves

together, because I am getting married today." The king smiled, and they went off to the ballroom.

Everyone was there, and King Joseph was ready to officiate. Zalem was waiting for his bride. First down the aisle walked Duke Luther and Rose. Second was Zion and Lillianna as the matron of honor and best man. Then Prince Victor walked down the aisle, with King Maxwell and Queen Julianna to help the ring bearer. Fourth were Zion and Lillianna's beautiful little girls, with the help of their grandmother Queen Tianna, as the flower girls. Finally, the doors shut and it was time for Isabelle to come down the aisle.

When Isabelle and Sir Nicholas got in front of the doors and were ready, he gave her a kiss and the doors opened. When Zalem saw his bride, a few tears fell out of his eyes because she was so beautiful. Isabelle wore simple pearl earrings and a silver necklace with small pearls encrusted in it. Her veil was a double-edge veil at chapel length, made of silk. Her hair was half up in a beautiful bump and the rest was curled and hanging. Throughout her hair there were little flowers. Her dress was a fishtail wedding dress that felt very silky, and had a lot of ruching. Her shoes were white and silver. Her makeup included a touch of midnight blue in her eye shadow. Isabelle looked amazing; better than Lillianna and Veronica.

Isabelle heard the music and continued down the aisle with her father by her side. She was so nervous, because she wasn't used to people starring at her. She finally reached the altar, where Sir Nicholas gave her a hug and a kiss and handed her off to Zalem. She wiped away his tears, which he tried to hide, and they smiled at each other. Then they continued to walk toward King Joseph, and he began to officiate.

Before they knew it, the ceremony was over and Zalem finally could kiss his bride. Everyone clapped and cheered, even the woman in the balcony that wore a blusher veil, and her name was Ilianna.

A Peek Into The Future...

Three years later, someone new is welcomed into Zaru, and her name is Gazelle. When Zalem and Gazelle meet, a lot of destruction happens that surpasses what Zalem has ever been through before. Zalem and Isabelle's marriage will be tested. Sadly, Zalem's entire family is torn apart when Gazelle enters the picture. Will he be able to mend his family together? There also is someone locked away in the dungeon below the Balcot castle. That person could stir up problems. All is never pure in the Eyes of Evil.

Book 2
Kingdoms of Magic
Eyes of Evil
#Whoisinthecell?

Go to

www.kingdomsofmagicseries.com and

enter this code to view the family tree.

Username: KingdomsOfMagic

Password: KOMTREE

All underlined letters are to be capitalized.

www.ingramcontent.com/pod-product-compliance
Lightning Source LLC
Chambersburg PA
CBHW031510040426

42445CB00009B/165